Preface

Microsoft Azure DevOps Engineer AZ 400: Microsoft Azure DevOps Engineer is a meticulously structured guide designed to equip professionals with the expertise required to implement DevOps practices using Microsoft Azure. As organizations increasingly adopt DevOps methodologies to enhance software development and operational efficiency, the role of an Azure DevOps Engineer has become essential in modern IT environments. This book provides a comprehensive framework to master key DevOps principles, including continuous integration and continuous delivery (CI/CD), infrastructure as code (IaC), source control management, security, compliance, and monitoring. Aligned with the objectives of the AZ-400 certification, the content systematically builds foundational knowledge before progressing to advanced concepts, ensuring that readers acquire both theoretical understanding and hands-on proficiency in designing and implementing DevOps strategies.

Beyond serving as an exam preparation resource, *Microsoft Certification AZ-400: Microsoft Azure DevOps Engineer* is an invaluable reference for professionals seeking to refine their skills in automating software development pipelines and managing cloud infrastructure efficiently. Each chapter integrates practical exercises, real-world case studies, and expert insights to reinforce learning and facilitate knowledge retention. Additionally, self-assessment tools, online test papers, and video tutorials provide an immersive learning experience, bridging the gap between theoretical concepts and real-world application. Whether you are an experienced DevOps professional aiming to validate your expertise or an IT specialist looking to transition into DevOps engineering, this book offers a structured and in-depth approach to mastering Azure DevOps practices, paving the way for career advancement in this dynamic and evolving field.

Table of Contents

Chapter 1: Practice Questions & Answers Part 1

QUESTION1

-

How should you confrere the release retention policy for the investment planning depletions suite? To answer, select the appropriate options in the answer area. NOTE: Each correct selection is worth one point.

Required secrets	Certificate
	Personal access token
	Shared access authorization token
	Username and password
Storage locations:	Azure Data Lake
	Azure Key Vault
	Azure Storage with HTTP access
	Azure storage with HTTPS access

A. Mastered
B. Not Mastered

Answer: A

QUESTION2

-

What should you use to implement the code quality restriction on the release pipeline for the investment planning applications suite?

A. a trigger
B. a pre deployment approval
C. a post-deployment approval
D. a deployment gate

Answer: D

QUESTION3

-

Your company creates a new Azure DevOps team. D18912E1457D5D1DDCBD40AB3BF70D5D You plan to use Azure DevOps for sprint planning.

You need to visualize the flow of your work by using an agile methodology. Which Azure DevOps component should you use?

A. Kanban boards
B. sprint planning
C. delivery plans
D. portfolio backlogs

Answer: A

QUESTION4

-

You have an Azure DevOps organization named Contoso that contains a project named Project 1. You provision an Azure key vault name Keyvault1. You need to reference Keyvault1 secrets in a build pipeline of Project1. What should you do first?

A. Create an XAML build service.
B. Create a variable group in Project1.
C. Add a secure file to Project1.
D. Configure the security policy of Contoso.
Answer: B

QUESTION5

-

You need to ensure that an Azure web app named az400-9940427-main can retrieve secrets from an Azure key vault named az400-9940427-kv1 by using a system managed identity.
The solution must use the principle of least privilege.
To complete this task, sign in to the Microsoft Azure portal.

A. Mastered
B. Not Mastered

Answer: A

QUESTION6

-

You are planning projects for three customers. Each customer's preferred process for work items is shown in the following table.

Customer name	Preferred process
Litware, Inc.	Track product backlog items (PBIs) and bugs on the Kanban board. Break the PBIs down into tasks on the task board.
Contoso, Ltd.	Track user stories and bugs on the Kanban board. Track the bugs and tasks on the task board.
A. Datum Corporation	Track requirements, change requests, risks, and reviews.

The customers all plan to use Azure DevOps for work item management.
Which work item process should you use for each customer? To answer, drag the appropriate work item process to the correct customers. Each work item process may be used once, more than once, or not at all. You may need to drag the split bar between panes or scroll to view content. NOTE: Each correct selection is worth one point.
A. Mastered
B. Not Mastered
Answer: A

QUESTION7

-

After you answer a **QUESTION** in this section, you will NOT be able to return to it. As a result, these **QUESTION**s will not appear in the review screen.
You have an Azure DevOps organization named Contoso and an Azure subscription. The subscription contains an Azure virtual machine scale set named VMSS1 that is configured for autoscaling.
You have a project in Azure DevOps named Project1. Project1 is used to build a web app named App1 and deploy App1 to VMSS1.
You need to ensure that an email alert is generated whenever VMSS1 scales in or out. Solution: From Azure Monitor, create an action group. Does this meet the goal?

A. Yes
B. No

Answer: B

QUESTION8

-

You use WhiteSource Bolt to scan a Node.js application.
The WhiteSource Bolt scan identifies numerous libraries that have invalid licenses. The libraries are used only during development and are not part of a production deployment.
You need to ensure that WhiteSource Bolt only scans production dependencies.
Which two actions should you perform? Each correct answer presents part of the solution. NOTE: Each correct selection is worth one point.

A. Run npm install and specify the --production flag.
B. Modify the WhiteSource Bolt policy and set the action for the licenses used by the development tools to Reassign.
C. Modify the devDependencies section of the project's Package.json file.
D. Configure WhiteSource Bolt to scan the node_modules directory only.

Answer: AC

QUESTION 9

-

You are developing an iOS application by using Azure DevOps.
You need to test the application manually on 10 devices without releasing the application to the public. Which two actions should you perform? Each correct answer presents part of the solution.
NOTE: Each correct selection is worth one point.
A. Create a Microsoft Intune device compliance policy.
B. Deploy a certificate from an internal certification authority (CA) to each device.
C. Register the application in the iTunes store.
D. Onboard the devices into Microsoft Intune.
E. Distribute a new release of the application.
F. Register the IDs of the devices in the Apple Developer portal.
Answer: BF

QUESTION 10

-

You have the following Azure policy.

```
If : (
  allef: {
        {
        field": "type".
          "equals":  "Microsoft. Storage/storage Accounts"
        },
        {
            "Field" : "Microsoft.storage/storageAccounts/SupportsHttpsTrafficonly",
"notEquals": "true"
}
        }
},
Then: {
Effect:"deny"
}
```

You assign the policy to the Tenant root group. What is the effect of the policy?

A. prevents all http traffic to existing Azure Storage accounts
B. ensures that all traffic to new Azure Storage accounts is encrypted
C. prevents HTTPS traffic to new Azure Storage accounts when the accounts are accessed over the Internet
D. ensures that all data for new Azure Storage accounts is encrypted at rest

Answer: B

QUESTION 11

-

You need to configure an Azure web app named az400-9940427-main to contain an environmental variable named "MAX_ITEMS". The environmental variable must have a value of 50.
To complete this task, sign in to the Microsoft Azure portal.

A. Mastered
B. Not Mastered

Answer: A

QUESTION 12

-

You are defining release strategies for two applications as shown in the following table.

Application name	Goal
Appl	Failure of Appl has a major impact on your company. You need a small group of users. who opted in to a testing Appl. to test new releases of the application.
App2	You need to minimize the time it takes to deploy new releases of App2. and you must be able to roll back as quickly as possible.

Which release strategy should you use for each application? To answer, drag the appropriate release strategies to the correct applications. Each release strategy may be used once, more than once, or not at all. You may need to drag the split bar between panes or scroll to view content.
NOTE: Each correct selection is worth one point.
A. Mastered
B. Not Mastered
Answer: A

QUESTION 13

-

Your company is building a new solution in Java.
The company currently uses a SonarQube server to analyze the code of .NET solutions. You need to analyze and monitor the code quality of the Java solution. Which task types should you add to the build pipeline?

A. Chef
B. Gradle
C. Octopus
D. Gulp

Answer: B

QUESTION 14

-

You are creating a NuGet package.
You plan to distribute the package to your development team privately. You need to share the package and test that the package can be consumed.

Which four actions should you perform in sequence? To answer, move the appropriate actions from the list of actions to the answer area and arrange them in the correct order.

Actions
Create a new Azure Artifacts feed.
Configure a self-hosted agent.
Publish a package.
Install a package.
Connect to an Azure Artifacts feed.

A. Mastered
B. Not Mastered

Answer: A

QUESTION 15

-

After you answer a **QUESTION** in this section, you will NOT be able to return to it. As a result, these **QUESTION**s will not appear in the review screen. You use Azure Pipelines to build and test a React js application. You have a pipeline that has a single job.
You discover thai installing JavaScript packages from npm takes approximately five minutes each time you run the pipeline. You need to recommend a solution to reduce the pipeline execution time.
Solution: You recommend defining a container job that uses a custom container that has the JavaScript packages preinstalled. Does this meet the goal?

A. Yes
B. No

Answer: B

QUESTION 16

-

After you answer a **QUESTION** in this section, you will NOT be able to return to it. As a result, these **QUESTION**s will not appear in the review screen.
You have an Azure DevOps organization named Contoso and an Azure subscription. The subscription contains an Azure virtual machine scale set named VMSS1 that is configured for autoscaling.

You have a project in Azure DevOps named Project1. Project1 is used to build a web app named App1 and deploy App1 to VMSS1.
You need to ensure that an email alert is generated whenever VMSS1 scales in or out. Solution: From Azure DevOps, configure the Notifications settings for Project1. Does this meet the goal?
A. Yes
B. No
Answer: A

QUESTION 17
-
Your company is building a new solution in Java.
The company currently uses a SonarQube server to analyze the code of .NET solutions. You need to analyze and monitor the code quality of the Java solution. Which task types should you add to the build pipeline?
A. Chef
B. Gradle
C. Octopus
D. Gulp
Answer: B

QUESTION 18
-
Your company uses Azure Artifacts for package management.
You need to configure an upstream source in Azure Artifacts for Python packages. Which repository type should you use as an upstream source?
A. PyPI
B. npmjs.org
C. Maven Central
D. third-party trusted Python
Answer: A

QUESTION 19
-
You have an Azure subscription that contains resources in several resource groups.
You need to design a monitoring strategy that will provide a consolidated view. The solution must support the following requirements:
• Support role-based access control (RBAC) by using Azure Active Directory (Azure AD) identities.
• Include visuals from Azure Monitor that are generated by using the Kusto query language.
• Support documentation written in markdown.
• Use the latest data available for each visual.
What should you use to create the consolidated view?
A. Azure Data Explorer
B. Azure dashboards
C. Azure Monitor
D. Microsoft Power Bl

Answer: A

QUESTION 20

-

You are designing a build pipeline in Azure Pipelines.
The pipeline requires a self-hosted agent. The build pipeline will run once daily and will take 30 minutes to complete. You need to recommend a compute type for the agent. The solution must minimize costs. What should you recommend?

A. Azure virtual machines
B. an Azure virtual machine scale set
C. an Azure Kubernetes Service (AKS) cluster
D. Azure Container Instances

Answer: B

QUESTION 21

-

You manage the Git repository for a large enterprise application.
During the development of the application, you use a file named Config.json.
You need to prevent Config.json from being committed to the source control whenever changes to the application are committed.
Which three actions should you perform in sequence? Mastered

A. Not Mastered

Answer: A

QUESTION 22

-

You are designing an Azure DevOps strategy for your company's development team. You suspect that the team's productivity is low due to accumulate technical debt. You need to recommend a metric to assess the amount of the team's technical debt. What should you recommend?

A. the number of code modules in an application
B. the number of unit test failures
C. the percentage of unit test failures
D. the percentage of overall time spent on rework

Answer: D

QUESTION 23

-

You have several apps that use an Azure SQL Database named db1.
You need to ensure that queries to db1 are tuned by Azure over time. The solution must only apply to db1. To complete this task, sign in to the Microsoft Azure

portal.

A. Mastered
B. Not Mastered

Answer: A

QUESTION 24

-

You have a build pipeline in Azure Pipelines that occasionally fails.
You discover that a test measuring the response time of an API endpoint causes the failures. You need to prevent the build pipeline from failing due to The test. Which two actions should you perform? Each correct answer presents part of the solution. NOTE: Each correct selection is worth one point

A. Enable Test Impact Analysis (TIA).
B. Enable test slicing.
C. Clear Flaky tests included in test pass percentage
D. Set Flaky test detection to Off
E. Manually mark the test as flaky.

Answer: CE

QUESTION 25

-

You have an Azure DevOps project that uses many package feeds.
You need to simplify the project by using a single feed that stores packages produced by your company and packages consumed from remote feeds. The solution must support public feeds and authenticated feeds.
What should you enable in DevOps?

A. Universal Packages
B. views in Azure Artifacts
C. upstream sources
D. a symbol server

Answer: B

QUESTION 26

-

You are building a Microsoft ASP.NET application that requires authentication. You need to authenticate users by using Azure Active Directory (Azure AD). What should you do first?

A. Create a membership database in an Azure SQL database.
B. Assign an enterprise application to users and groups.
C. Create an app registration in Azure AD.

D. Configure the application to use a SAML endpoint.
E. Create a new OAuth token from the application.

Answer: C

QUESTION 27

-

You need to execute inline testing of an Azure DevOps pipeline that uses a Docker deployment model. The solution must prevent the results from being published to the pipeline.
What should you use for the inline testing?

A. a single stage Dockerfile
B. an Azure Kubernetes Service (AKS) pod
C. a multi-stage Dockerfile
D. a Docker Compose file

Answer: C

QUESTION 28

-

Your company uses the following resources:
Windows Server 2019 container images hosted in an Azure Container Registry Azure virtual machines that run the latest version of Ubuntu An Azure
Log Analytics workspace Azure Active Directory (Azure AD) An Azure key vault
For which two resources can you receive vulnerability assessments in Azure Security Center? Each correct answer presents part of the solution.

A. the Azure Log Analytics workspace
B. the Azure key vault
C. the Azure virtual machines that run the latest version of Ubuntu
D. Azure Active Directory (Azure AD)
E. the Windows Server 2019 container images hosted in the Azure Container Registry

Answer: CE

QUESTION 29

-

You are designing YAML-based Azure pipelines for the apps shown in the following table.

Name	Platform	Release requirements
Appl	Azure virtual machine	Replace a fixed set of existing instances of the new version of the a in each iteration.
App2	Azure Kubernetes Service (AKS) cluster	Roll out a limited deployment of the new version of App2 to validate the functionality of the app. Once testing is successful. ex and the rollout.

You need to configure the YAML strategy value for each app. The solution must minimize app downtime. Which value should you configure for each app? To answer, select the appropriate options in the answer area. NOTE: Each correct selection is worth one point.

App1:	Canary
	Rolling
	runonce

App2:	Canary
	Rolling
	runonce

A. Mastered
B. Not Mastered

Answer: A

QUESTION 30

-

You are designing the security validation strategy for a project in Azure DevOps.
You need to identify package dependencies that have known security issues and can be resolved by an update. What should you use?

A. Octopus Deploy
B. Jenkins
C. Gradle
D. SonarQube

Answer: D

QUESTION 31

-

You have a web app that connects to an Azure SQL Database named db1.
You need to configure db1 to send Query Store runtime statistics to Azure Log Analytics. To complete this task, sign in to the Microsoft Azure portal.

A. Mastered
B. Not Mastered

Answer: A

QUESTION 32

-

Your company uses GitHub for source control. GitHub repositories store source code and store process documentation. The process documentation is saved as Microsoft Word documents that contain simple flow charts stored as .bmp files.

You need to optimize the integration and versioning of the process documentation and the flow charts. The solution must meet the following requirements:
• Store documents as plain text.
• Minimize the number of files that must be maintained.
• Simplify the modification, merging, and reuse of flow charts.
• Simplify the modification, merging, and reuse of documents.
What should you include in the solution? To answer, select the appropriate options in the answer area.
A. Mastered
B. Not Mastered

Answer: A

QUESTION 33

-

You are designing a configuration management solution to support five apps hosted on Azure App Service. Each app is available in the following three environments: development, test, and production.
You need to recommend a configuration management solution that meets the following requirements: Supports feature flags
Tracks configuration changes from the past 30 days Stores hierarchically structured configuration values
Controls access to the configurations by using role-based access control (RBAC) permission Stores shared values as key/value pairs that can be used by all the apps
Which Azure service should you recommend as the configuration management solution?
A. Azure Cosmos DB
B. Azure App Service
C. Azure App Configuration
D. Azure Key Vault
Answer: C

QUESTION 34

-

You have a multi-tier application. The front end of the application is hosted in Azure App Service. You need to identify the average load times of the application pages. What should you use?

A. the diagnostics logs of the App Service
B. Azure Application Insights
C. Azure Advisor
D. the activity log of the App Service

Answer: B

QUESTION 35

You have an Azure DevOps project named Project1 and an Azure subscription named Sub1. Sub1 contains an Azure virtual machine scale set named VMSS1. VMSS1 hosts a web application named WebApp1.
WebApp1 uses stateful sessions.
The WebApp1 installation is managed by using the Custom Script extension. The script resides in an Azure Storage account named sa1.
You plan to make a minor change to a UI element of WebApp1 and to gather user feedback about the change. You need to implement limited user testing for the new version of WebApp1 on VMSS1.
Which three actions should you perform? Each correct answer presents part of the solution. NOTE: Each correct selection is worth one point.

A. Modify the load balancer settings of VMSS1.
B. Redeploy VMSS1.
C. Upload a custom script file to sa1.
D. Modify the Custom Script extension settings of VMSS1.
E. Update the configuration of a virtual machine in VMSS1.

Answer: BCD

QUESTION 36

-

Your development team is building a new web solution by using the Microsoft Visual Studio integrated development environment (IDE).
You need to make a custom package available to all the developers. The package must be managed centrally, and the latest version must be available for consumption in Visual Studio automatically.
Which three actions should you perform? Each correct answer presents part of the solution. NOTE: Each correct selection is worth one point.

A. Publish the package to a feed.
B. Create a new feed in Azure Artifacts.
C. Upload a package to a Git repository.
D. Add the package URL to the Environment settings in Visual Studio.
E. Add the package URL to the NuGet Package Manager settings in Visual Studio.
F. Create a Git repository in Azure Repos.

Answer: ABE

QUESTION 37

-

Your company develops a client banking application that processes a large volume of data.
Code quality is an ongoing issue for the company. Recently, the code quality has deteriorated because of an increase in time pressure on the development team. You need to implement static code analysis.
During which phase should you use static code analysis?

A. build
B. production release
C. staging
D. integration testing
Answer: D

QUESTION 38

-

You plan to implement a CI/CD strategy for an Azure Web App named az400-11566895-main. You need to configure a staging environment for az400-11566895-main. To complete this task, sign in to the Microsoft Azure portal.

A. Mastered
B. Not Mastered

Answer: A

QUESTION 39

-

You need to increase the security of your team's development process.
Which type of security tool should you recommend for each stage of the development process? To answer, drag the appropriate security toots to the correct stages. Each security tool may be used once, more than once, or not at all. You may need to drag the split bar between panes or scroll to view content.

A. Mastered
B. Not Mastered

Answer: A

QUESTION 40

-

Your company has four projects. The version control requirements for each project are shown in the following table.

Project	Requirement
Project 1	Project leads must be able to restrict access to Individual files and folders in the repository
Project 2	The version control system must enforce the following rules before merging any changes to the main branch. • Changes must be reviewed by at least two project members. • Changes must be associated to at least one work team.
Project 3	The project members must be able to work In Azure Repos directly from Xode
Project 4	The release branch must only be viewable or editable by the project leads

You plan to use Azurc Rcpos for all the projects.
Which version control system should you use for each project? To answer, drag the appropriate version control systems to the correct projects. Each version control system may be used once, more than once, or not at all. You may need to drag the split bar between panes or scroll to view content.
NOTE: Each correct selection is worth one point.

A. Mastered
B. Not Mastered

Answer: A

QUESTION 41

-

Note: This question is part of a series of questions that present the same scenario. Each question in the series contains a unique solution that might meet the stated goals. Some question sets might have more than one correct solution, while others might not have a correct solution.
After you answer a question in this section, you will NOT be able to return to it. As a result, these questions will not appear in the review screen. You manage a project in Azure DevOps.
You need to prevent the configuration of the project from changing over time. Solution: Implement Continuous Assurance for the project. Does this meet the goal?

A. Yes
B. No

Answer: A

QUESTION 42

-

You have a web app hosted on Azure App Service. The web app stores data in an Azure SQL database. You need to generate an alert when there are 10,000 simultaneous connections to the database. The solution must minimize deve4opment effort.
Which option should you select in the Diagnostics settings of the database?

A. Send to Log Analytics
B. Archive to m storage account
C. Stream to an event hub

Answer: A

QUESTION 43

-

You have a free tier of an Azure DevOps organization named Contoso. Contoso contains 10 private projects. Each project has multiple jobs with no dependencies. You frequently run the jobs on five self-hosted agents but experience long build times and frequently queued builds.
You need to minimize the number of queued builds and the time it takes to run the builds. What should you do?

A. Purchase self-hosted parallel jobs.
B. Register additional self-hosted agents.
C. Purchase Microsoft-hosted parallel jobs.
D. Configure the pipelines to use the Microsoft-hosted agents.

Answer: A

QUESTION 44

-

After you answer a **QUESTION** in this section, you will NOT be able to return to it. As a result, these **QUESTION**s will not appear in the review screen. You use Azure Pipelines to build and test a React js application. You have a pipeline that has a single job.
You discover that installing JavaScript packages from npm takes approximately five minutes each time you run the pipeline.
You need to recommend a solution to reduce the pipeline execution time. Solution: You recommend enabling parallel jobs for the pipeline. Does this meet the goal?

A. Yes
B. No

Answer: B

QUESTION 45

-

You use Azure Artifacts to host NuGet packages that you create.
You need to make one of the packages available to anonymous users outside your organization. The solution must minimize the number of publication points. What should you do?

A. Create a new feed for the package
B. Publish the package to a public NuGet repository.
C. Promote the package to a release view.
D. Change the feed URL of the package.

Answer: A

QUESTION 46

-

You need to create and configure an Azure Storage account named az400lod11566895stor in a resource group named RG1lod11566895 to store the boot diagnostics for a virtual machine named VM1.
To complete this task, sign in to the Microsoft Azure portal.

A. Mastered
B. Not Mastered

Answer: A

QUESTION 47

-

Note: This question is part of a series of questions that present the same scenario. Each question in the series contains a unique solution that might meet the stated goals. Some question sets might have more than one correct solution, while others might not have a correct solution.
After you answer a question in this section, you will NOT be able to return to it. As a result, these questions will not appear in the review screen.
You plan to update the Azure DevOps strategy of your company.
You need to identify the following issues as they occur during the company's development process:
Licensing violations
Prohibited libraries
Solution: You implement continuous deployment. Does this meet the goal?

A. Yes
B. No

Answer: B

QUESTION 48

-

Note: This question is part of a series of questions that present the same scenario. Each question in the series contains a unique solution that might meet the stated goals. Some question sets might have more than one correct solution, while others might not have a correct solution.
After you answer a question in this section, you will NOT be able to return to it. As a result, these questions will not appear in the review screen.
You need to recommend an integration strategy for the build process of a Java application. The solution must meet the following requirements: The builds must access an on-premises dependency management system.
The build outputs must be stored as Server artifacts in Azure DevOps. The source code must be stored in a Git repository in Azure DevOps.
Solution: Configure an Octopus Tentacle on an on-premises machine. Use the Package Application task in the build pipeline.
Does this meet the goal?

A. Yes
B. No

Answer: A

QUESTION 49
-
Note: This question part of a series of questions that present the same scenario. Each question in the series contains a unique solution that might meet the stated goals. Some question sets might have more than one correct solution, while others might not have a correct solution
After you answer a question in this section, you will NOT be able to return to it. As a result these questions will not appear in the review screen.
You have an approval process that contains a condition. The condition requires that releases be approved by a team leader before they are deployed. You have a policy stating that approvals must occur within eight hours.
You discover that deployments fail if the approvals lake longer than two hours.
You need to ensure that the deployments only fail if the approvals take longer than eight hours.
Solution: From Pre-deployment conditions, you modify the Timeout setting for pre-deployment approvals. Does this meet the goal?

A. Yes
B. No

Answer: B

QUESTION 50
-
You need to create a notification if the peak average response time of an Azure web app named az400-9940427-main is more than five seconds when evaluated during a five-minute period. The notification must trigger the “https://contoso.com/notify” webhook.
To complete this task, sign in to the Microsoft Azure portal.

A. Mastered
B. Not Mastered

Answer: A

QUESTION 51

-

Note: This question is part of a series of questions that present the same scenario. Each question in the series contains a unique solution that might meet the stated goals. Some question sets might have more than one correct solution, while others might not have a correct solution.
After you answer a question in this section, you will NOT be able to return to it. As a result, these questions will not appear in the review screen. You need to recommend an integration strategy for the build process of a Java application. The solution must meet the following requirements:
The builds must access an on-premises dependency management system. The build outputs must be stored as Server artifacts in Azure DevOps.
The source code must be stored in a Git repository in Azure DevOps.
Solution: Configure the build pipeline to use a Hosted VS 2017 agent pool. Include the Java Tool Installer task in the build pipeline. Does this meet the goal?

A. Yes
B. No

Answer: B

QUESTION 52

-

Your company plans to use an agile approach to software development.
You need to recommend an application to provide communication between members of the development team who work in locations around the world. The applications must meet the following requirements:
Provide the ability to isolate the members of different project teams into separate communication channels and to keep a history of the chats within those channels.
Be available on Windows 10, Mac OS, iOS, and Android operating systems. Provide the ability to add external contractors and suppliers to projects.
Integrate directly with Azure DevOps. What should you recommend?

A. Microsoft Project
B. Bamboo
C. Microsoft Lync
D. Microsoft Teams

Answer: D

QUESTION 53

-

Note: This question is part of a series of questions **N**s that present the same scenario. Each question in the series contains a unique solution that might meet the stated goals. Some question sets might have more than one correct solution, while others might not have a correct solution.
After you answer a question in this section, you will NOT be able to return to it. As a result, these questions will not appear in the review screen.
The lead developer at your company reports that adding new application features takes longer than expected due to a large accumulated technical debt. You need to recommend changes to reduce the accumulated technical debt. Solution: You recommend increasing the test coverage.
Does this meet the goal?

A. Yes
B. No

Answer: B

QUESTION 54

-

Your company plans to use an agile approach to software development
You need to recommend an application to provide communication between members of the development team who work in locations around the world. The application must meet the following requirements:
• Provide the ability to isolate the members of efferent project teams into separate communication channels and to keep a history of the chats within those channels.
• Be available on Windows 10, Mac OS, iOS, and Android operating systems.
• Provide the ability to add external contractors and suppliers to projects.
• Integrate directly with Azure DevOps. What should you recommend?

A. Octopus
B. Bamboo
C. Microsoft Project
D. Slack

Answer: D

QUESTION 55

-

Your company is concerned that when developers introduce open source libraries, it creates licensing compliance issues.
You need to add an automated process to the build pipeline to detect when common open source libraries are added to the code base. What should you use?

A. Microsoft Visual SourceSafe
B. PDM
C. WhiteSource
D. OWASP ZAP

Answer: C

QUESTION 56
- (Exam Topic 3)
You add the virtual machines as managed nodes in Azure Automation State Configuration. You need to configure the computer in Group7. What should you do?

A. Run the Register-AzureRmAutomationDscNode Azure Powershell cmdlet.
B. Modify the ConfigurationMode property of the Local Configuration Manager (LCM).
C. Install PowerShell Core.
D. Modify the RefreshMode property of the Local Configuration Manager (LCM).

Answer: A

QUESTION 57
Note: This question is part of a series of questions that present the same scenario. Each question in the series contains a unique solution that might meet the stated goals. Some question sets might have more than one correct solution, while others might not have a correct solution.
After you answer a question in this section, you will NOT be able to return to it. As a result, these questions will not appear in the review screen.
Your company has a prefect in Azure DevOps for a new web application. You need to ensure that when code is checked in, a build runs automatically. Solution: from the Triggers tab of the build pipeline, you select Enable continuous integration
Does the meet the goal?

A. Yes
B. No

Answer: B

QUESTION 58
You need to recommend a Docker container build strategy that meets the following requirements
¡E Minimizes image sues
¡E Minimizes the security surface area of the final image What should you include m the recommendation?

A. multi-stage builds
B. single-stage builds
C. PowerShell Desired State Configuration (DSC)
D. Docker Swarm

Answer: A

QUESTION 59
You manage build pipelines and deployment pipelines by using Azure DevOps.
Your company has a team of 500 developers. New members are added continual lo the team

You need to automate me management of users and licenses whenever possible Which task must you perform manually?

A. modifying group memberships
B. procuring licenses
C. adding users
D. assigning entitlements

Answer: B

QUESTION 60
During a code review, you discover many quality issues. Many modules contain unused variables and empty catch Modes. You need to recommend a solution to improve the quality o' the code. What should you recommend?

A. In a Gradle build task, select Run Checkstyle.
B. In an Xcode build task, select Use xcpretty from Advanced
C. In a Grunt build task, select Enabled from Control Options.
D. In a Maven build task, select Run PM

Answer: D

QUESTION 61
Your company deploys applications m Docket containers.
You want to detect known explogts in the Docket images used to provision the Docker containers. You need to integrate image scanning into the application lifecycle. The solution must expose the explogts as early as possible during the application lifecycle. What should you configure?

A. a task executed in the continuous deployment pipeline and a scheduled task against a running production container.
B. a task executed in the continuous integration pipeline and a scheduled task that analyzes the production container.
C. a task executed in the continuous integration pipeline and a scheduled task that analyzes the image registry
D. manual tasks performed during the planning phase and the deployment phase

Answer: C

QUESTION 62
You have a brand policy in a project in Azure DevOps. The policy requires that code always builds successfully.
You need to ensure that a specific user can always merge change to the master branch, even if the code fails to compile. The solution must use the principle of least privilege.
What should you do?

A. From the Security setting of the repository, modify the access control tor the user.

B. From the Security settings of the branch, modify the access control for the user.
C. Add the user to the Build Administrators group,
D. Add the user to the Project Administrators group

Answer: B

QUESTION 63
Your company uses cloud-hosted Jenkins for builds.
You need to ensure that Jenkins can retrieve source code from Azure Repos. Which three actions should you perform? Each correct answer presents part of the solution
NOTE: Each correct answer selection is worth one point

A. Add the Team Foundation Server (TFS) plug-in to Jenkins.
B. Create a personal access token m your Azure DevOps account.
C. Create a webhook in Jenkins.
D. Add a domain to your Jenkins account.
E. Create a service hook m Azure DevOps.

Answer: ABE

QUESTION 64
You are developing an open source solution that uses a GitHub repository. You create a new public project in Azure DevOps. You plan to use Azure Pipelines for continuous build. The solution will use the GitHub Checks API.
Which authentication type should you use?

A. a personal access token
B. SAML
C. GrtHub App
D. OAuth

Answer: D

QUESTION 65
You use Azure Artifacts to host NuGet packages that you create.
You need to make one of the packages available to anonymous users outside your organization. The solution must minimize the number of publication points. What should you do?
A. Create a new feed for the package
B. Publish the package to a public NuGet repository.
C. Promote the package to a release view.
D. Change the feed URL of the packag

Answer: A

QUESTION 66

You have 50 Node.js-based projects that you scan by using WhiteSource. Each project includes Package.json, Package-lock.json, and Npm-shrinkwrap.json files. You need to minimize the number of libraries reports by WhiteSource to only the libraries that you explicitly reference. What should you do?

A. Configure the File System Agent plug in.
B. Delete Package lock.json.
C. Configure the Artifactory plug-in.
D. Add a devDependencies section to Package-lock.jso

Answer: D

QUESTION 67
Your company plans to use an agile approach to software development.
You need to recommend an application to provide communication between members of the development team who work in locations around the world. The applications must meet the following requirements:
„hProvide the ability to isolate the members of different project teams into separate communication channels and to keep a history of the chats within those channels.
„hBe available on Windows 10, Mac OS, iOS, and Android operating systems.
„hProvide the ability to add external contractors and suppliers to projects.
„hIntegrate directly with Azure DevOps. What should you recommend?

A. Microsoft Project
B. Bamboo
C. Microsoft Lync
D. Microsoft Teams

Answer: D

QUESTION 68
Your company develops an app for OS. All users of the app have devices that are members of a private distribution group in Microsoft Visual Studio App Center. You plan to distribute a new release of the app.
You need to identify which certificate file you require to distribute the new release from App Center. Which file type should you upload to App Center?

A. .cer
B. .pvk
C. .pfx
D. .p12

Answer: D

QUESTION 69

You need to implement the code flow strategy for Project2 in Azure DevOps. Which three actions should you perform in sequence? To answer, move the appropriate actions from the list of actions to the
answer area and arrange in the correct order.

Actions
Create a fork
Create a branch
Add a build validation policy
Add a build policy
Create a repository
Add an application access policy.

A. Mastered
B. Not Mastered
Answer: A

QUESTION 70

-

Where should the build and release agents for the investment planning application suite run? To answer, select the appropriate options in the answer area. NOTE: Each correct selection is worth one point.

Build agent.
A hosted service
A source control system
The developers' computers

Release agent.
A hosted service
A source control system
The developers' computers

A. Mastered
B. Not Mastered

Answer: A

QUESTION 71

-

What should you use to implement the code quality restriction on the release pipeline for the investment planning applications suite?

A. a trigger
B. a pre deployment approval
C. a post-deployment approval
D. a deployment gate

Answer: D

QUESTION 72

-

Your company creates a new Azure DevOps team. D18912E1457D5D1DDCBD40AB3BF70D5D
You plan to use Azure DevOps for sprint planning.
You need to visualize the flow of your work by using an agile methodology. Which Azure DevOps component should you use?

A. Kanban boards
B. sprint planning
C. delivery plans
D. portfolio backlogs

Answer: A

QUESTION 73

-

You plan to deploy a template named D:\Deploy.json to a resource group named Deploy-lod9940427. You need to modify the template to meet the following requirements, and then to deploy the template:
The address space must be reduced to support only 256 total IP addresses.
The subnet address space must be reduced to support only 64 total IP addresses. To complete this task, sign in to the Microsoft Azure portal.

A. Mastered
B. Not Mastered

Answer: A

QUESTION 74

-

You have an Azure DevOps organization named Contoso that contains a project named Project 1.
You provision an Azure key vault name Keyvault1. You need to reference Keyvault1 secrets in a build pipeline of Project1. What should you do first?

A. Create an XAML build service.
B. Create a variable group in Project1.

C. Add a secure file to Project1.

D. Configure the security policy of Contoso.

Answer: B

QUESTION 75

-

This question is part of a series of questions that present the same scenario. Each question in the series contains a unique solution that might meet the stated goals. Some question sets might have more than one correct solution, while others might not have a correct solution.
After you answer a question in this section, you will NOT be able to return to it. As a result, these questions will not appear in the review screen. You have an Azure DevOps project.
Your build process creates several artifacts.
You need to deploy the artifacts to on-premises servers.
Solution: You deploy an Azure self-hosted agent to an on-premises server. You add a Copy and Publish Build Artifacts task to the deployment pipeline. Does this meet the goal?

A. Yes
B. No

Answer: A

QUESTION 76

-

Your company develops an app for OS. All users of the app have devices that are members of a private distribution group in Microsoft Visual Studio App Center. You plan to distribute a new release of the app.
You need to identify which certificate file you require to distribute the new release from App Center. Which file type should you upload to App Center?

A. .cer
B. .pvk
C. .pfx
D. .p12

Answer: D

QUESTION 77

-

You plan to onboard 10 new developers.
You need to recommend a development environment that meets the following requirements:
Integrates with GitHub
Provides integrated debugging tools
Supports remote workers and hot-desking environments
Supports developers who use browsers, tablets, and Chromebooks What should you recommend?

A. VS Code
B. Xamarin Studio
C. MonoDevelop
D. Visual Studio Codespaces

Answer: D

QUESTION 78

-

Note: This question is part of * series of questions that present the same scenario. Each question in the series contains a unique solution that might meet the stated goals. Some question sett might have more than one correct solution, while others might not have a correct solution.
After you answer a question in this section, you will NOT be able to return to it. As a result, these questions will not appear in the review screen.
You have an approval process that contains a condition. The condition requires that releases be approved by a team leader before they are deployed. You have a poky stating that approvals must occur within eight hour.
You discover that deployments fail if the approvals take longer than two hours.
You need to ensure that the deployments only fail if the approvals take longer than eight hours.
Solution: From Post-deployment conditions, you modify the Time between re-evaluation of gates option. Does this meet the goal?
A. Yes
B. No

Answer: B

QUESTION 79

-

After you answer a question in this section, you will NOT be able to return to it. As a result, these questions will not appear in the review screen. You use Azure Pipelines to build and test a React js application. You have a pipeline that has a single job.
You discover thai installing JavaScript packages from npm takes approximately five minutes each time you run the pipeline. You need to recommend a solution to reduce the pipeline execution time.
Solution: You recommend defining a container job that uses a custom container that has the JavaScript packages preinstalled. Does this meet the goal?

A. Yes
B. No

Answer: B

QUESTION 80

-

You have a build pipeline in Azure Pipelines that uses different jobs to compile an application for 10 different architectures. The build pipeline takes approximately one day to complete. You need to reduce the time it takes to execute the build pipeline
Which two actions should you perform? Each correct answer presents part of the solution. NOTE: Each correct selection is worth one point

A. Move to a blue/green deployment pattern.
B. Create an agent pool.
C. Create a deployment group.
D. Reduce the size of the repository.
E. Increase the number of parallel jobs.

Answer: BE

QUESTION 81

-

You have an Azure DevOps organization named Contoso, an Azure DevOps project named Project1, an Azure subscription named Sub1, and an Azure key vault named vault1.
You need to ensure that you can reference the values of the secrets stored in vault1 in all the pipelines of Project1. The solution must prevent the values from being stored in the pipelines.
What should you do?

A. Create a variable group in Project1.
B. Add a secure file to Project1.
C. Modify the security settings of the pipelines.
D. Configure the security policy of Contoso.

Answer: A

QUESTION 82

-

Note: This question is part of a series of questions that present the same scenario. Each question in the series contains a unique solution that might meet the stated goals. Some question sets might have more than one correct solution, while others might not have a correct solution.
After you answer a question in this section, you win NOT be able to return to it. As a result, these questions win not appear in the review screen. You integrate a cloud- hosted Jenkins server and a new Azure DevOps deployment
You need Azure DevOps to send a notification to Jenkins when a developer commits changes to a branch in Azure Repos. Solution: You create a service hook subscription that uses the code pushed event. Does this meet the goal?

A. Yes
B. NO

Answer: A

QUESTION 83

-

Note: This question is part of a series of questions that present the same scenario. Each question in the series contains a unique solution that might meet the stated goals. Some question sets might have more than one correct solution, while others might not have a correct solution.
After you answer a question in this section, you will NOT be able to return to it. As a result, these questions will not appear in the review screen.
You plan to create a release pipeline that will deploy Azure resources by using Azure Resource Manager templates. The release pipeline will create the following resources:
Two resource groups
Four Azure virtual machines in one resource group Two Azure SQL databases in other resource group
You need to recommend a solution to deploy the resources.
Solution: Create two standalone templates, each of which will deploy the resources in its respective group. Does this meet the goal?

A. Yes
B. No

Answer: A

QUESTION 84

-

You have an Azure subscription that contains resources in several resource groups.
You need to design a monitoring strategy that will provide a consolidated view. The solution must support the following requirements:

• Support role-based access control (RBAC) by using Azure Active Directory (Azure AD) identities.
• Include visuals from Azure Monitor that are generated by using the Kusto query language.
• Support documentation written in markdown.
• Use the latest data available for each visual.

What should you use to create the consolidated view?

A. Azure Data Explorer
B. Azure dashboards
C. Azure Monitor
D. Microsoft Power Bl

Answer: A

QUESTION 85

-

You are designing a build pipeline in Azure Pipelines.
The pipeline requires a self-hosted agent. The build pipeline will run once daily and will take 30 minutes to complete. You need to recommend a compute type for the agent. The solution must minimize costs. What should you recommend?

A. Azure virtual machines
B. an Azure virtual machine scale set
C. an Azure Kubernetes Service (AKS) cluster
D. Azure Container Instances

Answer: B

QUESTION 86

-

You have an Azure DevOps project that contains a build pipeline. The build pipeline uses approximately 50 open source libraries. You need to ensure that all the open source libraries comply with your company's licensing standards. Which service should you use?

A. Ansible
B. Maven
C. WhiteSource Bolt
D. Helm

Answer: C

QUESTION 87

-

You are designing an Azure DevOps strategy for your company's development team. You suspect that the team's productivity is low due to accumulate technical debt. You need to recommend a metric to assess the amount of the team's technical debt. What should you recommend?

A. the number of code modules in an application
B. the number of unit test failures
C. the percentage of unit test failures
D. the percentage of overall time spent on rework

Answer: D

QUESTION 88

-

You have a GitHub repository.
You create a new repository in Azure DevOps.
You need to recommend a procedure to clone the repository from GitHub to Azure DevOps. What should you recommend?

A. Create a webhook.
B. Create a service connection for GitHub.
C. From Import a Git repository, click Import
D. Create a pull request.
E. Create a personal access token in Azure DevOps.

Answer: C

QUESTION 89

-

You have an Azure DevOps organization named Contoso.
You need to recommend an authentication mechanism that meets the following requirements:
• Supports authentication from Git
• Minimizes the need to provide credentials during authentication What should you recommend?

A. managed identities in Azure Active Directory (Azure AD)
B. personal access tokens (PATs) in Azure DevOps
C. user accounts in Azure Active Directory (Azure AD)
D. Alternate credentials in Azure DevOps

Answer: B

QUESTION 90

-

You are developing an application. The application source has multiple branches. You make several changes to a branch used for experimentation. You need to update the main branch to capture the changes made to the experimentation branch and override the history of the Git repository.
Which Git option should you use?

A. Rebase
B. Fetch
C. MergeD18912E1457D5D1DDCBD40AB3BF70D5D
D. Push

Answer: C

QUESTION 91

-

Your company uses the following resources:
Windows Server 2019 container images hosted in an Azure Container Registry Azure virtual machines that run the latest version of Ubuntu An Azure
Log Analytics workspace Azure Active Directory (Azure AD) An Azure key vault
For which two resources can you receive vulnerability assessments in Azure Security Center? Each correct answer presents part of the solution.

A. the Azure Log Analytics workspace
B. the Azure key vault
C. the Azure virtual machines that run the latest version of Ubuntu
D. Azure Active Directory (Azure AD)

E. the Windows Server 2019 container images hosted in the Azure Container Registry

Answer: CE

QUESTION 92

-

Your team uses an agile development approach.
You need to recommend a branching strategy for the team's Git repository. The strategy must meet the following requirements.
Provide the ability to work on multiple independent tasks in parallel. Ensure that checked-in code remains in a releasable state always. Ensure that new features can be abandoned at any time. Encourage experimentation. What should you recommend?

A. a single long-running branch
B. multiple long-running branches
C. a single fork per team member
D. a single-running branch with multiple short-lived topic branches

Answer: D

QUESTION 93

-

You have a project in Azure DevOps. You have an Azure Resource Group deployment project in Microsoft Visual Studio that is checked in to the Azure DevOps project.
You need to create a release pipeline that will deploy resources by using Azure Resource Manager templates. The solution must minimize administrative effort. Which task type should you include in the solution?

A. Azure Cloud Service Deployment
B. Azure RM Web App Deployment
C. Azure PowerShell
D. Azure App Service Manage

Answer: C

QUESTION 94

-

You have a web app that connects to an Azure SQL Database named db1.
You need to configure db1 to send Query Store runtime statistics to Azure Log Analytics. To complete this task, sign in to the Microsoft Azure portal.

A. Mastered
B. Not Mastered

Answer: A

QUESTION 95

-

You are designing a configuration management solution to support five apps hosted on Azure App Service. Each app is available in the following three environments: development, test, and production.

You need to recommend a configuration management solution that meets the following requirements: Supports feature flags

Tracks configuration changes from the past 30 days Stores hierarchically structured configuration values

Controls access to the configurations by using role-based access control (RBAC) permission Stores shared values as key/value pairs that can be used by all the apps

Which Azure service should you recommend as the configuration management solution?

A. Azure Cosmos DB
B. Azure App Service
C. Azure App Configuration
D. Azure Key Vault

Answer: C

QUESTION 96

-

Note: This question is part of a series of questions that present the same scenario. Each question in the series contains a unique solution that might meet the stated goals. Some question sets might have more than one correct solution, while others might not have a correct solution.

After you answer a question in this section, you will NOT be able to return to it. As a result, these questions will not appear in the review screen.

You have an approval process that contains a condition. The condition requires that releases be approved by a team leader before they are deployed. You have a policy stating that approvals must occur within eight hours.

You discover that deployment fail if the approvals take longer than two hours.

You need to ensure that the deployments only fail if the approvals take longer than eight hours.

Solution: From Post-deployment conditions, you modify the Timeout setting for post-deployment approvals. Does this meet the goal?

A. Yes
B. No

Answer: B

QUESTION 97

You have a multi-tier application. The front end of the application is hosted in Azure App Service. You need to identify the average load times of the application pages. What should you use?

A. the diagnostics logs of the App Service

B. Azure Application Insights
C. Azure Advisor
D. the activity log of the App Service

Answer: B

QUESTION 98

-

Note: This question is part of a series of questions that present the same scenario. Each question in the series contains a unique solution that might meet the stated goals. Some question sets might have more than one correct solution, while others might not have a correct solution.
After you answer a question in this section, you will NOT be able to return to it. As a result, these questions will not appear in the review screen. You manage a project in Azure DevOps.
You need to prevent the configuration of the project from changing over time. Solution: Perform a Subscription Health scan when packages are created. Does this meet the goal?

A. Yes
B. No

Answer: B

QUESTION 99

-

Your company develops a client banking application that processes a large volume of data.
Code quality is an ongoing issue for the company. Recently, the code quality has deteriorated because of an increase in time pressure on the development team. You need to implement static code analysis.
During which phase should you use static code analysis?

A. build
B. production release
C. staging
D. integration testing

Answer: D

QUESTION 100

-

You manage a website that uses an Azure SQL Database named db1 in a resource group named RG1lod11566895.
You need to modify the SQL database to protect against SQL injection. To complete this task, sign in to the Microsoft Azure portal.

A. Mastered
B. Not Mastered

Answer: A

QUESTION 101

-

You are developing an open source solution that uses a GitHub repository. You create a new public project in Azure DevOps.
You plan to use Azure Pipelines for continuous build. The solution will use the GitHub Checks API. Which authentication type should you use?

A. a personal access token
B. SAML
C. GitHub App
D. OAuth

Answer: C

QUESTION 102

-

You need to configure GitHub to use Azure Active Directory (Azure AD) for authentication. What should you do first?

A. Create a conditional access policy in Azure AD.
B. Modify the Security settings of the GitHub organization.
C. Create an Azure Active Directory B2C (Azure AD B2C) tenant.
D. Register GitHub in Azure AD.

Answer: D

QUESTION 103

-

You are finalizing a release in GitHub.
You need to apply the following labels to the release: Name
Email Release v3.0 Release date
How should you complete the git command? To answer, select the appropriate options in the answer area.
A. Mastered
B. Not Mastered

Answer: A

QUESTION 104

-

Your company develops an application named App1 that is deployed in production.
As part of an application update, a new service is being added to App1. The new service requires access to an application named App2 that is currently in development.

You need to ensure that you can deploy the update to App1 before App2 becomes available. You must be able to enable the service in App1 once App2 is deployed.
What should you do?

A. Create a branch in the build.
B. Implement a branch policy.
C. Create a fork in the build.
D. Implement a feature flag.

Answer: D

QUESTION 105

-

You plan to use Terraform to deploy an Azure resource group.
You need to install the required frameworks to support the planned deployment.
Which two frameworks should you install? Each correct answer presents part of the solution.
NOTE: Each correct selection is worth one point.

A. Vault
B. Terratest
C. Node.js
D. Yeoman
E. Tiller

Answer: BD

QUESTION 106

-

You need to configure a virtual machine named VM1 to securely access stored secrets in an Azure Key Vault named az400-11566895-kv. To complete this task, sign in to the Microsoft Azure portal.

A. Mastered
B. Not Mastered

Answer: A

QUESTION 107

-

Your company hosts a web application in Azure. The company uses Azure Pipelines for the build and release management of the application. Stakeholders report that the past few releases have negatively affected system performance. You configure alerts in Azure Monitor.
You need to ensure that new releases are only deployed to production if the releases meet defined performance baseline criteria in the staging environment first. What should you use to prevent the deployment of releases that fall to meet the performance baseline?

A. an Azure Scheduler job

B. a trigger
C. a gate
D. an Azure function

Answer: C

QUESTION 108

-

Note: This question is part of a series of questions that present the same scenario. Each question in the series contains a unique solution that might meet the stated goals. Some question sets might have more than one correct solution, while others might not have a correct solution.
After you answer a question in this section, you will NOT be able to return to it. As a result, these questions will not appear in the review screen.
Your company has a project in Azure DevOps for a new web application. You need to ensure that when code is checked in, a build runs automatically. Solution: From the Pre-deployment conditions settings of the release pipeline, you select After stage. Does this meet the goal?

A. Yes
B. No

Answer: B

QUESTION 109

-

You have an Azure DevOps organization named Contoso and an Azure subscription.
You use Azure DevOps to build and deploy a web app named App1. Azure Monitor is configured to generate an email notification in response to alerts generated whenever App1 generates a server-side error.
You need to receive notifications in Microsoft Teams whenever an Azure Monitor alert is generated. Which two actions should you perform? Each correct answer presents part of the solution.
NOTE: Each correct selection is worth one point.

A. Create an Azure logic app that has an HTTP request trigger.
B. Modify the Diagnostics settings in Azure Monitor.
C. Modify an action group in Azure Monitor.
D. Create an Azure Monitor workbook.
E. Create an Azure logic app that has an Azure DevOps trigger.

Answer: AB

QUESTION 110

-

Note: This question is part of a series of questions that present the same scenario. Each question in the series contains a unique solution that might meet the stated goals. Some question sets might have more than one correct solution, while others might not have a correct solution.

After you answer a question in this section, you will NOT be able to return to it. As a result, these questions will not appear in the review screen.
You have an approval process that contains a condition. The condition requires that releases be approved by a team leader before they are deployed. You have a policy stating that approvals must occur within eight hours.
You discover that deployment fail if the approvals take longer than two hours.
You need to ensure that the deployments only fail if the approvals take longer than eight hours.
Solution: From Pre-deployment conditions, you modify the Time between re-evaluation of gates option. Does this meet the goal?

A. Yes
B. No

Answer: B

QUESTION 111

-

After you answer a question in this section, you will NOT be able to return to it. As a result, these questions will not appear in the review screen. You use Azure Pipelines to build and test a React js application. You have a pipeline that has a single job.
You discover that installing JavaScript packages from npm takes approximately five minutes each time you run the pipeline.
You need to recommend a solution to reduce the pipeline execution time. Solution: You recommend enabling parallel jobs for the pipeline. Does this meet the goal'?

A. Yes
B. No

Answer: B

QUESTION 112

-

You have multi-tier application that h« an Azure Web Apps front end and art Azure SQL Datable back end. You need to recommend a solution to capture and store telemetry data. The solution must meet the following requirements:
• Support using ad-hoc queries to identify baselines.
• Trigger alerts when metrics in the baseline are exceeded.
• Store application and database metrics in a central location. What should you include in the recommendation?

A. Azure Application Insights
B. Azure SQL Database Intelligent Insights
C. Azure Event Hubs
D. Azure Log Analytics

Answer: A

QUESTION 113

-

Your company « concerned that when developers introduce open source Libraries, it creates licensing compliance issues.
You need to add an automated process to the build pipeline to detect when common open source libraries are added to the code base. What should you use?

A. Code Style
B. Microsoft Visual SourceSafe
C. Black Duck
D. Jenkins

Answer: C

QUESTION 114

-

You have an Azure Kubermets Service (AKS) implementation that is RBAC-enabled
You plan to use Azure Container Instances as a hosted development environment to run containers in the AKS implementation.
You need to conjure Azure Container Instances as a hosted environment for running me containers in AKS. Which three actions should you perform m sequence? To answer, move the appropriate actions from the list of actions to the answer area and arrange them in the correct order.

Actions
Run helm init.
Run az aks install—connector.
Create a file.
Run az role assignment create
Run kubectl apply.

A. Mastered
B. Not Mastered

Answer: A

QUESTION 115

-

Note: This question is part of a series of questions that present the same scenario. Each question in the series contains a unique solution that might meet the stated goals. Some question sets might have more than one correct solution, while others might not have a correct solution.

After you answer a question in this section, you will NOT be able to return to ft. As a result these questions will not appear in the review screen.
You company has a prefect in Azure DevOps for a new web application. You need to ensure that when code is checked in, a build runs automatically. Solution: From the Triggers tab of the build pipeline, you selected Batch changes while a build is in progress Does this meet the goal?

A. Yes
B. No

Answer: B

QUESTION 116

You plan to deploy a runbook that will create Azure AD user accounts.
You need to ensure that runbooks can run the Azure PowerShell cmdlets for Azure Active Directory. To complete this task, sign in to the Microsoft Azure portal.
A. Mastered
B. Not Mastered

Answer: A

QUESTION 117
-
You use Azure Artifacts to host NuGet packages that you create.
You need to make one of the packages available to anonymous users outside your organization. The solution must minimize the number of publication points. What should you do?

A. Create a new feed for the package
B. Publish the package to a public NuGet repository.
C. Promote the package to a release view.
D. Change the feed URL of the package.

Answer: A

QUESTION 118
-
Note: This question is part of a series of questions that present the same scenario. Each question in the series contains a unique solution that might meet the stated goals. Some question sets might have more than one correct solution, while others might not have a correct solution.
After you answer a question in this section, you will NOT be able to return to it. As a result, these questions will not appear in the review screen.
You plan to create a release pipeline that will deploy Azure resources by using Azure Resource Manager templates. The release pipeline will create the following resources:
Two resource groups
Four Azure virtual machines in one resource group Two Azure SQL databases in other resource group

You need to recommend a solution to deploy the resources.
Solution: Create a main template that will deploy the resources in one resource group and a nested template that will deploy the resources in the other resource
group.
Does this meet the goal?
A. Yes
B. No
Answer: B

QUESTION 119

-

You have a build pipeline in Azure Pipelines. You create a Slack App Integration.
You need to send build notifications to a Slack channel named #Development. What should you do first?
A. Configure a service connection.
B. Create a service hook subscription.
C. Create a project-level notification.
D. Create a global notification.
Answer: B

QUESTION 120

-

Note: This question is part of a series of questions that present the same scenario. Each question in the series contains a unique solution that might meet the stated goals. Some question sets might have more than one correct solution, while others might not have a correct solution.
After you answer a question in this section, you will NOT be able to return to it. As a result, these questions will not appear in the review screen.
You need to recommend an integration strategy for the build process of a Java application. The solution must meet the following requirements: The builds must access an on-premises dependency management system.
The build outputs must be stored as Server artifacts in Azure DevOps. The source code must be stored in a Git repository in Azure DevOps.
Solution: Configure an Octopus Tentacle on an on-premises machine. Use the Package Application task in the build pipeline.
Does this meet the goal?
A. Yes
B. No
Answer: A

QUESTION 121

-

Your company hosts a web application in Azure. The company uses Azure Pipelines for the build and release management of the application. Stakeholders report that the past few releases have negatively affected system performance. You configure alerts in Azure Monitor.

You need to ensure that new releases are only deployed to production if the releases meet defined performance baseline criteria in the staging environment first What should you use to prevent the deployment of releases that fail to meet the performance baseline?
A. a trigger
B. an Azure function
C. a gate
D. an Azure Scheduler job
Answer: C

QUESTION 122
-
You have 50 Node.js-based projects that you scan by using WhiteSource. Each project includes Package.json, Package-lock.json, and Npm-shrinkwrap.json files. You need to minimize the number of libraries reports by WhiteSource to only the libraries that you explicitly reference.
What should you do?

A. Configure the File System Agent plug in.
B. Delete Package lock.json.
C. Configure the Artifactory plug-in.
D. Add a devDependencies section to Package-lock.json.

Answer: D

QUESTION 123
-
You have an application that consists of several Azure App Service web apps and Azure functions.
You need to access the security of the web apps and the functions.
Which Azure features can you use to provide a recommendation for the security of the application?

A. Security & Compliance in Azure Log Analytics
B. Resource health in Azure Service Health
C. Smart Detection in Azure Application Insights
D. Compute & apps in Azure Security Center

Answer: D

QUESTION 124
-
You need to create a notification if the peak average response time of an Azure web app named az400-9940427-main is more than five seconds when evaluated during a five-minute period. The notification must trigger the "https://contoso.com/notify" webhook.
To complete this task, sign in to the Microsoft Azure portal.

A. Mastered
B. Not Mastered

Answer: A

QUESTION 125

-

Your company plans to use an agile approach to software development.
You need to recommend an application to provide communication between members of the development team who work in locations around the world. The applications must meet the following requirements:
Provide the ability to isolate the members of different project teams into separate communication channels and to keep a history of the chats within those channels.
Be available on Windows 10, Mac OS, iOS, and Android operating systems. Provide the ability to add external contractors and suppliers to projects.
Integrate directly with Azure DevOps. What should you recommend?

A. Microsoft Project
B. Bamboo
C. Microsoft Lync
D. Microsoft Teams

Answer: D

QUESTION 126

-

Your company uses Service Now for incident management. You develop an application that runs on Azure.

The company needs to generate a ticket in Service Now when the application fails to authenticate. Which Azure Log Analytics solution should you use?

A. Automation & Control

B. IT Service Management Connector (ITSM)

C. Application lmiQ.hu Connector

D. insight & Analytics

Answer: B

QUESTION 127

-

Note: This question is part of a series of questions that present the same scenario. Each question in the series contains a unique solution that might meet the stated goals. Some question sets might have more than one correct solution, while others might not have a correct solution.

After you answer a question in this section, you will NOT be able to return to it. As a result, these questions will not appear in the review screen.

The lead developer at your company reports that adding new application features takes longer than expected due to a large accumulated technical debt. You need to recommend changes to reduce the accumulated technical debt. Solution: You recommend reducing the code complexity.

Does this meet the goal?

A. Yes

B. No

Answer: A

QUESTION 128

-

You have a private GitHub repository.

You need to display the commit status of the repository on Azure Boards. What should you do first?

A. Create a GitHub action in GitHub.

B. Add the Azure Pipelines app to the GitHub repository.

C. Configure multi-factor authentication (MFA) for your GitHub account.

D. Add the Azure Boards app to the repository.

Answer: D

QUESTION 129

- (Exam Topic 3)

In Azure DevOps, you create Project3.

You need to meet the requirements of the project. What should you do first?

A. From Azure DevOps, create a service endpoint.
B. From SonarQube, obtain an authentication token.
C. From Azure DevOps, modify the build definition.
D. From SonarQube, create a project.
Answer: A

QUESTION 130
Note: This question is part of a series of questions that present the same scenario. Each question in the series contains a unique solution that might meet the stated goals. Some question sets might have more than one correct solution, while others might not have a correct solution.
After you answer a question in this section, you will NOT be able to return to it. As a result, these questions will not appear in the review screen.
Your company has a prefect in Azure DevOps for a new web application. You need to ensure that when code is checked in, a build runs automatically. Solution: from the Triggers tab of the build pipeline, you select Enable continuous integration
Does the meet the goal?
A. Yes
B. No
Answer: B

QUESTION 131
You need to recommend a Docker container build strategy that meets the following requirements
¡E Minimizes image sues
¡E Minimizes the security surface area of the final image What should you include m the recommendation?

A. multi-stage builds
B. single-stage builds
C. PowerShell Desired State Configuration (DSC)
D. Docker Swarm
Answer: A

QUESTION 132
You manage build pipelines and deployment pipelines by using Azure DevOps.
Your company has a team of 500 developers. New members are added continual lo the team
You need to automate me management of users and licenses whenever possible Which task must you perform manually?
A. modifying group memberships
B. procuring licenses
C. adding users
D. assigning entitlements
Answer: B

QUESTION 133

During a code review, you discover many quality issues. Many modules contain unused variables and empty catch Modes. You need to recommend a solution to improve the quality o' the code. What should you recommend?
A. In a Gradle build task, select Run Checkstyle.
B. In an Xcode build task, select Use xcpretty from Advanced
C. In a Grunt build task, select Enabled from Control Options.
D. In a Maven build task, select Run PM
Answer: D

QUESTION 134
Your company deploys applications m Docket containers.
You want to detect known explogts in the Docket images used to provision the Docker containers. You need to integrate image scanning into the application lifecycle. The solution must expose the explogts as early as possible during the application lifecycle. What should you configure?
A. a task executed in the continuous deployment pipeline and a scheduled task against a running production container.
B. a task executed in the continuous integration pipeline and a scheduled task that analyzes the production container.
C. a task executed in the continuous integration pipeline and a scheduled task that analyzes the image registry
D. manual tasks performed during the planning phase and the deployment phase

Answer: C

QUESTION 135
You have a brand policy in a project in Azure DevOps. The policy requires that code always builds successfully.
You need to ensure that a specific user can always merge change to the master branch, even if the code fails to compile. The solution must use the principle of least privilege.
What should you do?
A. From the Security setting of the repository, modify the access control tor the user.
B. From the Security settings of the branch, modify the access control for the user.
C. Add the user to the Build Administrators group,
D. Add the user to the Project Administrators group
Answer: B

QUESTION 136
Your company uses cloud-hosted Jenkins for builds.
You need to ensure that Jenkins can retrieve source code from Azure Repos. Which three actions should you perform? Each correct answer presents part of the solution
NOTE: Each correct answer selection is worth one point

A. Add the Team Foundation Server (TFS) plug-in to Jenkins.
B. Create a personal access token m your Azure DevOps account.
C. Create a webhook in Jenkins.
D. Add a domain to your Jenkins account.

E. Create a service hook m Azure DevOps.
Answer: ABE

QUESTION 137
You are developing an open source solution that uses a GitHub repository. You create a new public project in Azure DevOps. You plan to use Azure Pipelines for continuous build. The solution will use the GitHub Checks API.
Which authentication type should you use?
A. a personal access token
B. SAML
C. GrtHub App
D. OAuth
Answer: D

QUESTION 138
You use Azure Artifacts to host NuGet packages that you create.
You need to make one of the packages available to anonymous users outside your organization. The solution must minimize the number of publication points. What should you do?
A. Create a new feed for the package
B. Publish the package to a public NuGet repository.
C. Promote the package to a release view.
D. Change the feed URL of the packag
Answer: A

QUESTION 140
You have 50 Node.js-based projects that you scan by using WhiteSource. Each project includes Package.json, Package-lock.json, and Npm-shrinkwrap.json files. You need to minimize the number of libraries reports by WhiteSource to only the libraries that you explicitly reference.
What should you do?
A. Configure the File System Agent plug in.
B. Delete Package lock.json.
C. Configure the Artifactory plug-in.
D. Add a devDependencies section to Package-lock.jso
Answer: D

QUESTION 141
Your company plans to use an agile approach to software development.
You need to recommend an application to provide communication between members of the development team who work in locations around the world. The applications must meet the following requirements:
„hProvide the ability to isolate the members of different project teams into separate communication channels and to keep a history of the chats within those channels.
„hBe available on Windows 10, Mac OS, iOS, and Android operating systems.
„hProvide the ability to add external contractors and suppliers to projects.
„hIntegrate directly with Azure DevOps. What should you recommend?
A. Microsoft Project

B. Bamboo
C. Microsoft Lync
D. Microsoft Teams
Answer: D
QUESTION 142
Your company develops an app for OS. All users of the app have devices that are members of a private distribution group in Microsoft Visual Studio App Center. You plan to distribute a new release of the app.
You need to identify which certificate file you require to distribute the new release from App Center. Which file type should you upload to App Center?

A. .cer
B. .pvk
C. .pfx
D. .p12
Answer: D

QUESTION 143
Note: This question part of a series of questions that present the same scenario. Each question in the series contains a unique solution that might meet the staled goals. Some question sets might have more than one correct solution, whale others might not have a correct solution.
After you answer a question in this section, you will NOT be able to return to It. As a result, these questions will not appear in the review screen.
You integrate a cloud-hosted Jenkins server and a new Azure DevOps depsoyment. You need Azure DevOps to send a notification to Jenkins when a developer commits changes to a branch in Azure Repos.
Solution: You add a trigger to the build pipeline. Does this meet the goal?
A. Yes
B. NO
Answer: B

QUESTION 144
Note: This question is part of * series of questions that present the same scenario. Each question in the series contains a unique solution that might meet the stated
goals. Some question sett might have more than one correct solution, while others might not have a correct solution.
After you answer a question in this section, you will NOT be able to return to it. As a result, these questions will not appear in the review screen.
You have an approval process that contains a condition. The condition requires that releases be approved by a team leader before they are deployed. You have a poky stating that approvals must occur within eight hour.
You discover that deployments fail if the approvals take longer than two hours. You need to ensure that the deployments only fail if the approvals take longer than eight hours.
Solution: From Post-deployment conditions, you modify the Time between reevaluation of gates option. Does this meet the goal?
A. Yes

B. No
Answer: B

QUESTION 145
Note: This question n part of a series of questions that present the same scenario. Each question in the series contains a unique solution that might meet the stated goals. Some question sets might have more than one correct solution, while others might not have a correct solution
After you answer a question in this section, you will NOT be able to return to it. As a result these questions will not appear in the review screen.
You have an approval process that contains a condition. The condition requires that releases be approved by a team leader before they are deployed. You have a policy stating that approvals must occur within eight hours.
You discover that deployments fail if the approvals lake longer than two hours. You need to ensure that the deployments only fail if the approvals take longer than eight hours.
Solution: From Pre-deployment conditions, you modify the Timeout setting for predeployment approvals. Does this meet the goal?
A. Yes
B. No
Answer: B

QUESTION 146
Your company has a hybrid cloud between Azure and Azure Stack.
The company uses Azure DevOps for its CI/CD pipelines. Some applications are built by using Erlang and Hack.
You need to ensure that Erlang and Hack are supported as part of the build strategy across the hybrid cloud. The solution must minimize management overhead. What should you use to execute the build pipeline?

A. AzureDevOps self-hosted agents on Azure DevTest Labs virtual machines.
B. AzureDevOps self-hosted agents on virtual machine that run on Azure Stack
C. AzureDevOps self-hosted agents on Hyper-V virtual machines
D. a Microsoft-hosted agent
Answer: B

QUESTION 147
Your company builds a multi-tier web application.
You use Azure DevOps and host the production application on Azure virtual machines.
Your team prepares an Azure Resource Manager template of the virtual machine that you mil use to test new features. You need to create a staging environment in Azure that meets the following requirements:
¡E Minimizes the cost of Azure hosting
¡E Provisions the virtual machines automatically
¡E Use the custom Azure Resource Manager template to provision the virtual machines What should you do?

A. In Azure DevOps, configure new tasks in the release pipeline to create and delete the virtual machines m Azure DevTest Labs.
B. From Azure Cloud Shell, run Azure PowerShell commands to create and delete the new virtual machines in a staging resource group.
C. In Azure DevOps, configure new tasks in the release pipeline to deploy to Azure Cloud Services.
D. In Azure Cloud Shell, run Azure CLI commands to create and delete the new virtual machines in a staging resource group.
Answer: A

QUESTION 148
Your company plans to use an agile approach to software development You need to recommend an application to provide communication between members of the development team who work in locations around the world. The
application must meet the following requirements:
¡E Provide the ability to isolate the members of efferent project teams into separate communication channels and to keep a history of the chats within those channels.
¡E Be available on Windows 10, Mac OS, iOS, and Android operating systems.
¡E Provide the ability to add external contractors and suppliers to projects.
¡E Integrate directly with Azure DevOps. What should you recommend?
A. Octopus
B. Bamboo
C. Microsoft Project
D. Slack
Answer: D

QUESTION 149
Your company uses Azure DevOps for the build pipelines and deployment pipelines of Java based projects. You need to recommend a strategy for managing technical debt.
Which two actions should you include in the recommendation? Each correct answer presents part of the solution NOTE: Each correct selection is worth one point.

A. Integrate Azure DevOps and SonarQube.
B. Integrates Azure DevOPs and Azure DevTest Labs.
C. Configure post-deployment approvals in the deployment pipeline.
D. Configure pre-deployment approvals in the deployment pipelin
Answer: AC

QUESTION 150
Your company has an on-premises Bitbucket Server that is used for Git-based source control. The server is protected by a firewall that blocks inbound Internet traffic.
You plan to use Azure DevOps to manage the build and release processes Which two components are required to integrate Azure DevOps and Bitbucket? Each correct answer presents part of the solution.
NOTE: Each correct selection is worth one port.
A. an External Git service connection
B. a Microsoft hosted agent

C. service hooks
D. a self- hosted agent
E. a deployment M group
Answer: AD

QUESTION 151
Note: This question is part of a series of questions that present the same scenario. Each question in the series contains a unique solution that might meet the stated goals. Some question sets might have more than one correct solution, while others might not have a correct solution.
After you answer a question in this section, you will NOT be able to return to it. As a result, these questions will not appear in the review screen.
Your company has a project in Azure DevOps for a new web application. You need to ensure that when code is checked in, a build runs automatically. Solution: From the Pre-deployment conditions settings of the release pipeline, you select After stage.
Does this meet the goal?
A. Yes
B. No
Answer: B

QUESTION 152
Note: This question is part of a series of questions that present the same scenario. Each question in the series contains a unique solution that might meet the stated goals. Some question sets might have more than one correct solution, while others might not have a correct solution.
After you answer a question in this section, you will NOT be able to return to it. As a result, these questions will not appear in the review screen.
Your company has a project in Azure DevOps for a new web application. You need to ensure that when code is checked in, a build runs automatically. Solution: From the Pre-deployment conditions settings of the release pipeline, you select Batch changes while a build is in progress.
Does this meet the goal?
A. Yes
B. No
Answer: B

QUESTION 153
Note: This question is part of a series of questions that present the same scenario. Each question in the series contains a unique solution that might meet the stated goals. Some question sets might have more than one correct solution, while others might not have a correct solution.
After you answer a question in this section, you will NOT be able to return to it. As a result, these questions will not appear in the review screen.
You have an approval process that contains a condition. The condition requires that releases be approved by a team leader before they are deployed. You have a policy stating that approvals must occur within eight hours.
You discover that deployment fail if the approvals take longer than two hours. You need to ensure that the deployments only fail if the approvals take longer than eight hours.
Solution: From Pre-deployment conditions, you modify the Time between reevaluation of gates option. Does this meet the goal?

A. Yes
B. No
Answer: A

QUESTION 154
Your company is concerned that when developers introduce open source libraries, it creates licensing compliance issues.
You need to add an automated process to the build pipeline to detect when common open source libraries are added to the code base. What should you use?
A. Microsoft Visual SourceSafe
B. PDM
C. WhiteSource
D. OWASP ZAP
Answer: C

QUESTION 155
Note: This question is part of a series of questions that present the same scenario. Each question in the series contains a unique solution that might meet the stated goals. Some question sets might have more than one correct solution, while others might not have a correct solution.
After you answer a question in this section, you will NOT be able to return to it. As a result, these questions will not appear in the review screen.
You integrate a cloud-hosted Jenkins server and a new Azure DevOps deployment. You need Azure DevOps to send a notification to Jenkins when a developer commits
changes to a branch in Azure Repos.
Solution: You create a service hook subscription that uses the build completed event Does this meet the goal?
A. Yes
B. No
Answer: A

QUESTION 156
Your company hosts a web application in Azure. The company uses Azure Pipelines for the build and release management of the application. Stakeholders report that the past few releases have negatively affected system performance.
You configure alerts in Azure Monitor.
You need to ensure that new releases are only deployed to production if the releases meet defined performance baseline criteria in the staging environment first What should you use to prevent the deployment of releases that fail to meet the performance baseline?
A. a trigger
B. an Azure function
C. a gate
D. an Azure Scheduler job
Answer: C

QUESTION 157

Your company is building a mobile app that targets Android devices and OS devices. Your team uses Azure DevOps to manage all work items and release cycles. You need to recommend a solution to perform the following tasks
¡E Collect crash reports for issue analysis
¡E Distribute beta releases to your testers.
¡E Get user feedback on the functionality of new apps. What should you include in the recommendation?
A. Jenkins integration
B. Azure Application Insights widgets
C. the Microsoft Test & Feedback extension
D. Microsoft Visual Studio App Center integration
Answer: D
QUESTION 158
You have a GitHub repository.
You create a new repository in Azure DevOps.
You need to recommend a procedure to clone the repository from GitHub to Azure DevOps. What should you recommend?
A. Create a webhook.
B. Create a service connection for GitHub.
C. From Import a Git repository, click Import
D. Create a pull request.
E. Create a personal access token in Azure DevOp
Answer: C

QUESTION 159
To resolve the current technical issue, what should you do to the Register-AzureRmAutomationDscNode command?
A. Change the value of the ConfigurationMode parameter.
B. Replace the Register-AzureRmAutomationDscNode cmdlet with Register-AzureRmAutomationScheduledRunbook
C. Add the AllowModuleOverwrite parameter.
D. Add the DefaultProfile parameter.
Answer: A

QUESTION 160
-
What should you use to implement the code quality restriction on the release pipeline for the investment planning applications suite?
A. a trigger
B. a pre deployment approval
C. a post-deployment approval
D. a deployment gate
Answer: D

QUESTION 161
-

Your company creates a new Azure DevOps team. D18912E1457D5D1DDCBD40AB3BF70D5D
You plan to use Azure DevOps for sprint planning.
You need to visualize the flow of your work by using an agile methodology. Which Azure DevOps component should you use?
A. Kanban boards
B. sprint planning
C. delivery plans
D. portfolio backlogs
Answer: A

QUESTION 162
-
You have an Azure DevOps organization named Contoso that contains a project named Project 1. You provision an Azure key vault name Keyvault1. You need to reference Keyvault1 secrets in a build pipeline of Project1. What should you do first?
A. Create an XAML build service.
B. Create a variable group in Project1.
C. Add a secure file to Project1.
D. Configure the security policy of Contoso.
Answer: B

QUESTION 163
-
You need to ensure that an Azure web app named az400-9940427-main can retrieve secrets from an Azure key vault named az400-9940427-kv1 by using a system managed identity.
The solution must use the principle of least privilege.
To complete this task, sign in to the Microsoft Azure portal.
A. Mastered
B. Not Mastered
Answer: A

QUESTION 164
-
After you answer a question in this section, you will NOT be able to return to it. As a result, these questions will not appear in the review screen.
You have an Azure DevOps organization named Contoso and an Azure subscription. The subscription contains an Azure virtual machine scale set named VMSS1 that is configured for autoscaling.
You have a project in Azure DevOps named Project1. Project1 is used to build a web app named App1 and deploy App1 to VMSS1.
You need to ensure that an email alert is generated whenever VMSS1 scales in or out. Solution: From Azure Monitor, create an action group. Does this meet the goal?
A. Yes
B. No
Answer: B

QUESTION 165

-

You use WhiteSource Bolt to scan a Node.js application.
The WhiteSource Bolt scan identifies numerous libraries that have invalid licenses. The libraries are used only during development and are not part of a production deployment.
You need to ensure that WhiteSource Bolt only scans production dependencies.
Which two actions should you perform? Each correct answer presents part of the solution. NOTE: Each correct selection is worth one point.
A. Run npm install and specify the --production flag.
B. Modify the WhiteSource Bolt policy and set the action for the licenses used by the development tools to Reassign.
C. Modify the devDependencies section of the project's Package.json file.
D. Configure WhiteSource Bolt to scan the node_modules directory only.
Answer: AC

QUESTION 166

-

You are developing an iOS application by using Azure DevOps.
You need to test the application manually on 10 devices without releasing the application to the public. Which two actions should you perform? Each correct answer presents part of the solution. NOTE: Each correct selection is worth one point.
A. Create a Microsoft Intune device compliance policy.
B. Deploy a certificate from an internal certification authority (CA) to each device.
C. Register the application in the iTunes store.
D. Onboard the devices into Microsoft Intune.
E. Distribute a new release of the application.
F. Register the IDs of the devices in the Apple Developer portal.
Answer: BF

QUESTION 167

-

You need to configure an Azure web app named az400-9940427-main to contain an environmental variable named "MAX_ITEMS". The environmental variable must have a value of 50.
To complete this task, sign in to the Microsoft Azure portal.
A. Mastered
B. Not Mastered
Answer: A

QUESTION 168

-

Your company is building a new solution in Java.
The company currently uses a SonarQube server to analyze the code of .NET solutions. You need to analyze and monitor the code quality of the Java solution. Which task types should you add to the build pipeline?
A. Chef

B. Gradle
C. Octopus
D. Gulp
Answer: B

QUESTION 169

-

After you answer a question in this section, you will NOT be able to return to it. As a result, these questions will not appear in the review screen. You use Azure Pipelines to build and test a React js application. You have a pipeline that has a single job.
You discover thai installing JavaScript packages from npm takes approximately five minutes each time you run the pipeline. You need to recommend a solution to reduce the pipeline execution time.
Solution: You recommend defining a container job that uses a custom container that has the JavaScript packages preinstalled. Does this meet the goal?
A. Yes
B. No
Answer: B

QUESTION 170

-

After you answer a question in this section, you will NOT be able to return to it. As a result, these questions will not appear in the review screen.
You have an Azure DevOps organization named Contoso and an Azure subscription. The subscription contains an Azure virtual machine scale set named VMSS1 that is configured for autoscaling.
You have a project in Azure DevOps named Project1. Project1 is used to build a web app named App1 and deploy App1 to VMSS1.
You need to ensure that an email alert is generated whenever VMSS1 scales in or out. Solution: From Azure DevOps, configure the Notifications settings for Project1. Does this meet the goal?
A. Yes
B. No

Answer: A

QUESTION 171

-

Your company is building a new solution in Java.
The company currently uses a SonarQube server to analyze the code of .NET solutions. You need to analyze and monitor the code quality of the Java solution. Which task types should you add to the build pipeline?

A. Chef
B. Gradle
C. Octopus
D. Gulp

Answer: B

QUESTION 172

-

Your company uses Azure Artifacts for package management.

You need to configure an upstream source in Azure Artifacts for Python packages. Which repository type should you use as an upstream source?

A. PyPI

B. npmjs.org

C. Maven Central

D. third-party trusted Python

Answer: A

QUESTION 173

-

You have an Azure subscription that contains resources in several resource groups.

You need to design a monitoring strategy that will provide a consolidated view. The solution must support the following requirements:

• Support role-based access control (RBAC) by using Azure Active Directory (Azure AD) identities.

• Include visuals from Azure Monitor that are generated by using the Kusto query language.

• Support documentation written in markdown.

• Use the latest data available for each visual.

What should you use to create the consolidated view?

A. Azure Data Explorer

B. Azure dashboards

C. Azure Monitor

D. Microsoft Power Bl

Answer: A

QUESTION 174

-

You are designing a build pipeline in Azure Pipelines.

The pipeline requires a self-hosted agent. The build pipeline will run once daily and will take 30 minutes to complete. You need to recommend a compute type for the agent. The solution must minimize costs. What should you recommend?

A. Azure virtual machines

B. an Azure virtual machine scale set

C. an Azure Kubernetes Service (AKS) cluster

D. Azure Container Instances

Answer: B

QUESTION 175

-

You are designing an Azure DevOps strategy for your company's development team. You suspect that the team's productivity is low due to accumulate technical debt. You need to recommend a metric to assess the amount of the team's technical debt. What should you recommend?
A. the number of code modules in an application
B. the number of unit test failures
C. the percentage of unit test failures
D. the percentage of overall time spent on rework
Answer: D

QUESTION 176
-
You have several apps that use an Azure SQL Database named db1.
You need to ensure that queries to db1 are tuned by Azure over time. The solution must only apply to db1. To complete this task, sign in to the Microsoft Azure portal.
A. Mastered
B. Not Mastered
Answer: A

QUESTION 177
-
You have a build pipeline in Azure Pipelines that occasionally fails.
You discover that a test measuring the response time of an API endpoint causes the failures. You need to prevent the build pipeline from failing due to The test. Which two actions should you perform? Each correct answer presents part of the solution. NOTE: Each correct selection is worth one point
A. Enable Test Impact Analysis (TIA).
B. Enable test slicing.
C. Clear Flaky tests included in test pass percentage
D. Set Flaky test detection to Off
E. Manually mark the test as flaky.
Answer: CE

QUESTION 178
-
You have an Azure DevOps project that uses many package feeds.
You need to simplify the project by using a single feed that stores packages produced by your company and packages consumed from remote feeds. The solution must support public feeds and authenticated feeds.
What should you enable in DevOps?
A. Universal Packages
B. views in Azure Artifacts
C. upstream sources
D. a symbol server
Answer: B

QUESTION 179

-
You are building a Microsoft ASP.NET application that requires authentication. You need to authenticate users by using Azure Active Directory (Azure AD). What should you do first?
A. Create a membership database in an Azure SQL database.
B. Assign an enterprise application to users and groups.
C. Create an app registration in Azure AD.
D. Configure the application to use a SAML endpoint.
E. Create a new OAuth token from the application.
Answer: C

QUESTION 180
-
You need to execute inline testing of an Azure DevOps pipeline that uses a Docker deployment model. The solution must prevent the results from being published

to the pipeline.
What should you use for the inline testing?
A. a single stage Dockerfile
B. an Azure Kubernetes Service (AKS) pod
C. a multi-stage Dockerfile
D. a Docker Compose file
Answer: C

QUESTION 181
-
Your company uses the following resources:
Windows Server 2019 container images hosted in an Azure Container Registry Azure virtual machines that run the latest version of Ubuntu An Azure
Log Analytics workspace Azure Active Directory (Azure AD) An Azure key vault
For which two resources can you receive vulnerability assessments in Azure Security Center? Each correct answer presents part of the solution.
A. the Azure Log Analytics workspace
B. the Azure key vault
C. the Azure virtual machines that run the latest version of Ubuntu
D. Azure Active Directory (Azure AD)
E. the Windows Server 2019 container images hosted in the Azure Container Registry
Answer: CE

QUESTION 182
-
You are designing the security validation strategy for a project in Azure DevOps.
You need to identify package dependencies that have known security issues and can be resolved by an update. What should you use?
A. Octopus Deploy
B Jenkins
C. Gradle

D. SonarQube
Answer: D

QUESTION 183

-

You have a web app that connects to an Azure SQL Database named db1.
You need to configure db1 to send Query Store runtime statistics to Azure Log Analytics. To complete this task, sign in to the Microsoft Azure portal.
A. Mastered
B. Not Mastered
Answer: A

QUESTION 184

-

You are designing a configuration management solution to support five apps hosted on Azure App Service. Each app is available in the following three environments: development, test, and production.
You need to recommend a configuration management solution that meets the following requirements: Supports feature flags
Tracks configuration changes from the past 30 days Stores hierarchically structured configuration values
Controls access to the configurations by using role-based access control (RBAC) permission Stores shared values as key/value pairs that can be used by all the apps
Which Azure service should you recommend as the configuration management solution?
A. Azure Cosmos DB
B. Azure App Service
C. Azure App Configuration
D. Azure Key Vault
Answer: C

QUESTION 185

-

You have a multi-tier application. The front end of the application is hosted in Azure App Service. You need to identify the average load times of the application pages. What should you use?
A. the diagnostics logs of the App Service
B. Azure Application Insights
C. Azure Advisor
D. the activity log of the App Service
Answer: B

QUESTION 186

-

You have an Azure DevOps project named Project1 and an Azure subscription named Sub1. Sub1 contains an Azure virtual machine scale set named VMSS1. VMSS1 hosts a web application named WebApp1.
WebApp1 uses stateful sessions.

The WebApp1 installation is managed by using the Custom Script extension. The script resides in an Azure Storage account named sa1.
You plan to make a minor change to a UI element of WebApp1 and to gather user feedback about the change. You need to implement limited user testing for the new version of WebApp1 on VMSS1.
Which three actions should you perform? Each correct answer presents part of the solution. NOTE: Each correct selection is worth one point.
A. Modify the load balancer settings of VMSS1.
B. Redeploy VMSS1.
C. Upload a custom script file to sa1.
D. Modify the Custom Script extension settings of VMSS1.
E. Update the configuration of a virtual machine in VMSS1.
Answer: BCD

QUESTION 187
-
Your development team is building a new web solution by using the Microsoft Visual Studio integrated development environment (IDE).
You need to make a custom package available to all the developers. The package must be managed centrally, and the latest version must be available for consumption in Visual Studio automatically.
Which three actions should you perform? Each correct answer presents part of the solution. NOTE: Each correct selection is worth one point.

A. Publish the package to a feed.
B. Create a new feed in Azure Artifacts.
C. Upload a package to a Git repository.
D. Add the package URL to the Environment settings in Visual Studio.
E. Add the package URL to the NuGet Package Manager settings in Visual Studio.
F. Create a Git repository in Azure Repos.
Answer: ABE

QUESTION 188
-
Your company develops a client banking application that processes a large volume of data.
Code quality is an ongoing issue for the company. Recently, the code quality has deteriorated because of an increase in time pressure on the development team. You need to implement static code analysis.
During which phase should you use static code analysis?
A. build
B. production release
C. staging
D. integration testing
Answer: D

QUESTION 189
-

You plan to implement a CI/CD strategy for an Azure Web App named az400-11566895-main. You need to configure a staging environment for az400-11566895-main. To complete this task, sign in to the Microsoft Azure portal.
A. Mastered
B. Not Mastered
Answer: A

QUESTION 190
-
Note: This question is part of a series of questions that present the same scenario. Each question in the series contains a unique solution that might meet the stated goals. Some question sets might have more than one correct solution, while others might not have a correct solution.
After you answer a question in this section, you will NOT be able to return to it. As a result, these questions will not appear in the review screen.
You manage a project in Azure DevOps.
You need to prevent the configuration of the project from changing over time. Solution: Implement Continuous Assurance for the project. Does this meet the goal?
A. Yes
B. No
Answer: A

QUESTION 191
-
You have a web app hosted on Azure App Service. The web app stores data in an Azure SQL database. You need to generate an alert when there are 10,000 simultaneous connections to the database. The solution must minimize deve4opment effort.
Which option should you select in the Diagnostics settings of the database?
A. Send to Log Analytics
B. Archive to m storage account
C. Stream to an event hub
Answer: A

QUESTION 192
-
You have a free tier of an Azure DevOps organization named Contoso. Contoso contains 10 private projects. Each project has multiple jobs with no dependencies. You frequently run the jobs on five self-hosted agents but experience long build times and frequently queued builds.
You need to minimize the number of queued builds and the time it takes to run the builds. What should you do?
A. Purchase self-hosted parallel jobs.
B. Register additional self-hosted agents.
C. Purchase Microsoft-hosted parallel jobs.
D. Configure the pipelines to use the Microsoft-hosted agents.
Answer: A

QUESTION 193

-
After you answer a question in this section, you will NOT be able to return to it. As a result, these questions will not appear in the review screen. You use Azure Pipelines to build and test a React js application. You have a pipeline that has a single job.
You discover that installing JavaScript packages from npm takes approximately five minutes each time you run the pipeline.
You need to recommend a solution to reduce the pipeline execution time. Solution: You recommend enabling parallel jobs for the pipeline. Does this meet the goal?
A. Yes
B. No
Answer: B
A. Mastered
B. Not Mastered
Answer: A

QUESTION 194
-
You use Azure Artifacts to host NuGet packages that you create.
You need to make one of the packages available to anonymous users outside your organization. The solution must minimize the number of publication points. What should you do?
A. Create a new feed for the package
B. Publish the package to a public NuGet repository.
C. Promote the package to a release view.
D. Change the feed URL of the package.
Answer: A

QUESTION 195
-
You need to create and configure an Azure Storage account named az400lod11566895stor in a resource group named RG1lod11566895 to store the boot diagnostics for a virtual machine named VM1.
To complete this task, sign in to the Microsoft Azure portal.
A. Mastered
B. Not Mastered
Answer: A

QUESTION 196
-
Note: This question is part of a series of questions that present the same scenario. Each question in the series contains a unique solution that might meet the stated goals. Some question sets might have more than one correct solution, while others might not have a correct solution.
After you answer a question in this section, you will NOT be able to return to it. As a result, these questions will not appear in the review screen.
You plan to update the Azure DevOps strategy of your company.
You need to identify the following issues as they occur during the company's development process:
Licensing violations

Prohibited libraries
Solution: You implement continuous deployment. Does this meet the goal?
A. Yes
B. No
Answer: B

QUESTION 197
-
Note: This question is part of a series of questions that present the same scenario. Each question in the series contains a unique solution that might meet the stated goals. Some question sets might have more than one correct solution, while others might not have a correct solution.
After you answer a question in this section, you will NOT be able to return to it. As a result, these questions will not appear in the review screen.
You need to recommend an integration strategy for the build process of a Java application. The solution must meet the following requirements: The builds must access an on-premises dependency management system.
The build outputs must be stored as Server artifacts in Azure DevOps. The source code must be stored in a Git repository in Azure DevOps.
Solution: Configure an Octopus Tentacle on an on-premises machine. Use the Package Application task in the build pipeline.
Does this meet the goal?
A. Yes
B. No
Answer: A

QUESTION 198
-
Note: This question is part of a series of questions that present the same scenario. Each question in the series contains a unique solution that might meet the stated goals. Some question sets might have more than one correct solution, while others might not have a correct solution.
After you answer a question in this section, you will NOT be able to return to it. As a result, these questions will not appear in the review screen.
You have an approval process that contains a condition. The condition requires that releases be approved by a team leader before they are deployed. You have a policy stating that approvals must occur within eight hours.
You discover that deployments fail if the approvals lake longer than two hours.
You need to ensure that the deployments only fail if the approvals take longer than eight hours.
Solution: From Pre-deployment conditions, you modify the Timeout setting for pre-deployment approvals. Does this meet the goal?
A. Yes
B. No
Answer: B

QUESTION 199
-
You need to create a notification if the peak average response time of an Azure web app named

az400-9940427-main is more than five seconds when evaluated during a five-minute period. The notification must trigger the "https://contoso.com/notify" webhook.
To complete this task, sign in to the Microsoft Azure portal.
A. Mastered
B. Not Mastered
Answer: A

QUESTION 200
-
Note: This question is part of a series of questions that present the same scenario. Each question in the series contains a unique solution that might meet the stated goals. Some question sets might have more than one correct solution, while others might not have a correct solution.
After you answer a question in this section, you will NOT be able to return to it. As a result, these questions will not appear in the review screen.
You need to recommend an integration strategy for the build process of a Java application. The solution must meet the following requirements:
The builds must access an on-premises dependency management system. The build outputs must be stored as Server artifacts in Azure DevOps.
The source code must be stored in a Git repository in Azure DevOps.
Solution: Configure the build pipeline to use a Hosted VS 2017 agent pool. Include the Java Tool Installer task in the build pipeline. Does this meet the goal?
A. Yes
B. No
Answer: B

QUESTION 201
-
Your company plans to use an agile approach to software development.
You need to recommend an application to provide communication between members of the development team who work in locations around the world. The applications must meet the following requirements:
Provide the ability to isolate the members of different project teams into separate communication channels and to keep a history of the chats within those channels.
Be available on Windows 10, Mac OS, iOS, and Android operating systems. Provide the ability to add external contractors and suppliers to projects.
Integrate directly with Azure DevOps. What should you recommend?
A. Microsoft Project
B. Bamboo
C. Microsoft Lync
D. Microsoft Teams
Answer: D

QUESTION 202
-

Note: This question is part of a series of questions that present the same scenario. Each question in the series contains a unique solution that might meet the stated goals. Some question sets might have more than one correct solution, while others might not have a correct solution.
After you answer a question in this section, you will NOT be able to return to it. As a result, these questions will not appear in the review screen.
The lead developer at your company reports that adding new application features takes longer than expected due to a large accumulated technical debt. You need to recommend changes to reduce the accumulated technical debt. Solution: You recommend increasing the test coverage.
Does this meet the goal?
A. Yes
B. No
Answer: B

QUESTION 203
-
Your company plans to use an agile approach to software development
You need to recommend an application to provide communication between members of the development team who work in locations around the world. The application must meet the following requirements:
• Provide the ability to isolate the members of efferent project teams into separate communication channels and to keep a history of the chats within those channels.
• Be available on Windows 10, Mac OS, iOS, and Android operating systems.
• Provide the ability to add external contractors and suppliers to projects.
• Integrate directly with Azure DevOps. What should you recommend'?
A. Octopus
B. Bamboo
C. Microsoft Project
D. Slack
Answer: D

QUESTION 204
-
Your company is concerned that when developers introduce open source libraries, it creates licensing compliance issues.
You need to add an automated process to the build pipeline to detect when common open source libraries are added to the code base. What should you use?
A. Microsoft Visual SourceSafe
B. PDM
C. WhiteSource
D. OWASP ZAP
Answer: C

QUESTION 205
-(Exam Topic 3)
You add the virtual machines as managed nodes in Azure Automation State Configuration. You need to configure the computer in Group7. What should you do?

A. Run the Register-AzureRmAutomationDscNode Azure Powershell cmdlet.
B. Modify the ConfigurationMode property of the Local Configuration Manager (LCM).
C. Install PowerShell Core.
D. Modify the RefreshMode property of the Local Configuration Manager (LCM).
Answer: A

QUESTION 206
Note: This question is part of a series of questions that present the same scenario. Each question in the series contains a unique solution that might meet the stated goals. Some question sets might have more than one correct solution, while others might not have a correct solution.
After you answer a question in this section, you will NOT be able to return to it. As a result, these questions will not appear in the review screen.
Your company has a prefect in Azure DevOps for a new web application. You need to ensure that when code is checked in, a build runs automatically. Solution: from the Triggers tab of the build pipeline, you select Enable continuous integration
Does the meet the goal?
A. Yes
B. No
Answer: B

QUESTION 207
You need to recommend a Docker container build strategy that meets the following requirements
¡E Minimizes image sues
¡E Minimizes the security surface area of the final image What should you include m the recommendation?
A. multi-stage builds
B. single-stage builds
C. PowerShell Desired State Configuration (DSC)
D. Docker Swarm
Answer: A

QUESTION 208
You manage build pipelines and deployment pipelines by using Azure DevOps.
Your company has a team of 500 developers. New members are added continual lo the team
You need to automate me management of users and licenses whenever possible Which task must you perform manually?
A. modifying group memberships
B. procuring licenses
C. adding users
D. assigning entitlements
Answer: B

QUESTION 209
During a code review, you discover many quality issues. Many modules contain unused variables and empty catch Modes. You need to recommend a solution to improve the quality o' the code. What should you recommend?

A. In a Gradle build task, select Run Checkstyle.
B. In an Xcode build task, select Use xcpretty from Advanced
C. In a Grunt build task, select Enabled from Control Options.
D. In a Maven build task, select Run PM
Answer: D

QUESTION 210
Your company deploys applications m Docket containers.
You want to detect known explogts in the Docket images used to provision the Docker containers. You need to integrate image scanning into the application lifecycle. The solution must expose the explogts as early as possible during the application lifecycle. What should you configure?
A. a task executed in the continuous deployment pipeline and a scheduled task against a running production container.
B. a task executed in the continuous integration pipeline and a scheduled task that analyzes the production container.
C. a task executed in the continuous integration pipeline and a scheduled task that analyzes the image registry
D. manual tasks performed during the planning phase and the deployment phase
Answer: C

QUESTION 211
You have a brand policy in a project in Azure DevOps. The policy requires that code always builds successfully.
You need to ensure that a specific user can always merge change to the master branch, even if thc code fails to compile. The solution must use the principle of least privilege.
What should you do?
A. From the Security setting of the repository, modify the access control tor the user.
B. From the Security settings of the branch, modify the access control for the user.
C. Add the user to the Build Administrators group,
D. Add the user to the Project Administrators group
Answer: B

QUESTION 212
Your company uses cloud-hosted Jenkins for builds.
You need to ensure that Jenkins can retrieve source code from Azure Repos. Which three actions should you perform? Each correct answer presents part of the solution
NOTE: Each correct answer selection is worth one point
A. Add the Team Foundation Server (TFS) plug-in to Jenkins.
B. Create a personal access token m your Azure DevOps account.
C. Create a webhook in Jenkins.
D. Add a domain to your Jenkins account.
E. Create a service hook m Azure DevOps.
Answer: ABE

QUESTION 213

You are developing an open source solution that uses a GitHub repository. You create a new public project in Azure DevOps. You plan to use Azure Pipelines for continuous build. The solution will use the GitHub Checks API.
Which authentication type should you use?
A. a personal access token
B. SAML
C. GrtHub App
D. OAuth
Answer: D

QUESTION 214
You use Azure Artifacts to host NuGet packages that you create.
You need to make one of the packages available to anonymous users outside your organization. The solution must minimize the number of publication points. What should you do?
A. Create a new feed for the package
B. Publish the package to a public NuGet repository.
C. Promote the package to a release view.
D. Change the feed URL of the package
Answer: A

QUESTION 215
You have 50 Node.js-based projects that you scan by using WhiteSource. Each project includes Package.json, Package-lock.json, and Npm-shrinkwrap.json files. You need to minimize the number of libraries reports by WhiteSource to only the libraries that you explicitly reference.
What should you do?
A. Configure the File System Agent plug in.
B. Delete Package lock.json.
C. Configure the Artifactory plug-in.
D. Add a devDependencies section to Package-lock.jso
Answer: D

QUESTION 216
Your company plans to use an agile approach to software development.
You need to recommend an application to provide communication between members of the development team who work in locations around the world. The applications must meet the following requirements:
„hProvide the ability to isolate the members of different project teams into separate communication channels and to keep a history of the chats within those channels.
„hBe available on Windows 10, Mac OS, iOS, and Android operating systems.
„hProvide the ability to add external contractors and suppliers to projects.
„hIntegrate directly with Azure DevOps. What should you recommend?
A. Microsoft Project
B. Bamboo
C. Microsoft Lync
D. Microsoft Teams
Answer: D

QUESTION 217

Your company develops an app for OS. All users of the app have devices that are members of a private distribution group in Microsoft Visual Studio App Center. You plan to distribute a new release of the app.

You need to identify which certificate file you require to distribute the new release from App Center. Which file type should you upload to App Center?

A. .cer

B. .pvk

C. .pfx

D. .p12

Answer: D

QUESTION 218

-

Which branching strategy should you recommend for the investment planning applications suite?

A. release isolation

B. main only

C. development isolation

D. feature isolation

Answer: C

QUESTION 219

-

What should you use to implement the code quality restriction on the release pipeline for the investment planning applications suite?

A. a trigger

B. a pre deployment approval

C. a post-deployment approval

D. a deployment gate

Answer: D

QUESTION 220

-

Your company creates a new Azure DevOps team. D18912E1457D5D1DDCBD40AB3BF70D5D

You plan to use Azure DevOps for sprint planning.

You need to visualize the flow of your work by using an agile methodology. Which Azure DevOps component should you use?

A. Kanban boards

B. sprint planning

C. delivery plans

D. portfolio backlogs

Answer: A

QUESTION 221

-

You plan to deploy a template named D:\Deploy.json to a resource group named Deploy-lod9940427. You need to modify the template to meet the following requirements, and then to deploy the template:
The address space must be reduced to support only 256 total IP addresses.
The subnet address space must be reduced to support only 64 total IP addresses. To complete this task, sign in to the Microsoft Azure portal.
A. Mastered
B. Not Mastered
Answer: A

QUESTION 222
-
You have an Azure DevOps organization named Contoso that contains a project named Project 1. You provision an Azure key vault name Keyvault1. You need to reference Keyvault1 secrets in a build pipeline of Project1. What should you do first?
A. Create an XAML build service.
B. Create a variable group in Project1.
C. Add a secure file to Project1.
D. Configure the security policy of Contoso.
Answer: B

QUESTION 223
-
This question is part of a series of questions that present the same scenario. Each question in the series contains a unique solution that might meet the stated goals. Some question sets might have more than one correct solution, while others might not have a correct solution.
After you answer a question in this section, you will NOT be able to return to it. As a result, these questions will not appear in the review screen.You have an Azure DevOps project.
Your build process creates several artifacts.
You need to deploy the artifacts to on-premises servers.
Solution: You deploy an Azure self-hosted agent to an on-premises server. You add a Copy and Publish Build Artifacts task to the deployment pipeline. Does this meet the goal?
C. Yes
D. No
Answer: A

QUESTION 224
-
You plan to onboard 10 new developers.
You need to recommend a development environment that meets the following requirements:
Integrates with GitHub
Provides integrated debugging tools
Supports remote workers and hot-desking environments
Supports developers who use browsers, tablets, and Chromebooks What should you recommend?
A. VS Code
B. Xamarin Studio

C. MonoDevelop
D. Visual Studio Codespaces
Answer: D

QUESTION 225
-
Note: This question is part of a series of questions that present the same scenario. Each question in the series contains a unique solution that might meet the stated goals. Some question sets might have more than one correct solution, while others might not have a correct solution.
After you answer a question in this section, you will NOT be able to return to it. As a result, these questions will not appear in the review screen.
You have an approval process that contains a condition. The condition requires that releases be approved by a team leader before they are deployed. You have a poky stating that approvals must occur within eight hour.
You discover that deployments fail if the approvals take longer than two hours.
You need to ensure that the deployments only fail if the approvals take longer than eight hours.
Solution: From Post-deployment conditions, you modify the Time between re-evaluation of gates option. Does this meet the goal?
A. Yes
B. No
Answer: B

QUESTION 226
-
After you answer a question in this section, you will NOT be able to return to it. As a result, these questions will not appear in the review screen. You use Azure Pipelines to build and test a React js application. You have a pipeline that has a single job.
You discover thai installing JavaScript packages from npm takes approximately five minutes each time you run the pipeline. You need to recommend a solution to reduce the pipeline execution time.
Solution: You recommend defining a container job that uses a custom container that has the JavaScript packages preinstalled. Does this meet the goal?
A. Yes
B. No
Answer: B

QUESTION 227
-
You have a build pipeline in Azure Pipelines that uses different jobs to compile an application for 10 different architectures. The build pipeline takes approximately one day to complete. You need to reduce the time it takes to execute the build pipeline
Which two actions should you perform? Each correct answer presents part of the solution. NOTE: Each correct selection is worth one point
A. Move to a blue/green deployment pattern.
B. Create an agent pool.
C. Create a deployment group.
D. Reduce the size of the repository.

E. Increase the number of parallel jobs.
Answer: BE

QUESTION 228

-

You have an Azure DevOps organization named Contoso, an Azure DevOps project named Project1, an Azure subscription named Sub1, and an Azure key vault named vault1.
You need to ensure that you can reference the values of the secrets stored in vault1 in all the pipelines of Project1. The solution must prevent the values from being stored in the pipelines.
What should you do?
A. Create a variable group in Project1.
B. Add a secure file to Project1.
C. Modify the security settings of the pipelines.
D. Configure the security policy of Contoso.
Answer: A

QUESTION 229

-

Note: This question is part of a series of questions that present the same scenario. Each question in the series contains a unique solution that might meet the stated goals. Some question sets might have more than one correct solution, while others might not have a correct solution.
After you answer a question in this section, you will NOT be able to return to it. As a result, these questions will not appear in the review screen.
You plan to create a release pipeline that will deploy Azure resources by using Azure Resource Manager templates. The release pipeline will create the following resources:
Two resource groups
Four Azure virtual machines in one resource group Two Azure SQL databases in other resource group
You need to recommend a solution to deploy the resources.
Solution: Create two standalone templates, each of which will deploy the resources in its respective group. Does this meet the goal?
A. Yes
B. No
Answer: A

QUESTION 230

-

You have an Azure subscription that contains resources in several resource groups.
You need to design a monitoring strategy that will provide a consolidated view. The solution must support the following requirements:
• Support role-based access control (RBAC) by using Azure Active Directory (Azure AD) identities.
• Include visuals from Azure Monitor that are generated by using the Kusto query language.
• Support documentation written in markdown.
• Use the latest data available for each visual.
What should you use to create the consolidated view?

A. Azure Data Explorer
B. Azure dashboards
C. Azure Monitor
D. Microsoft Power Bl
Answer: A

QUESTION 231

-

You are designing a build pipeline in Azure Pipelines.
The pipeline requires a self-hosted agent. The build pipeline will run once daily and will take 30 minutes to complete. You need to recommend a compute type for the agent. The solution must minimize costs. What should you recommend?
A. Azure virtual machines
B. an Azure virtual machine scale set
C. an Azure Kubernetes Service (AKS) cluster
D. Azure Container Instances
Answer: B

QUESTION 232

-

You have an Azure DevOps project that contains a build pipeline. The build pipeline uses approximately 50 open source libraries. You need to ensure that all the open source libraries comply with your company's licensing standards. Which service should you use?
A. Ansible
B. Maven
C. WhiteSource Bolt
D. Helm
Answer: C

QUESTION 233

-

You are designing an Azure DevOps strategy for your company's development team. You suspect that the team's productivity is low due to accumulate technical debt. You need to recommend a metric to assess the amount of the team's technical debt. What should you recommend?
A. the number of code modules in an application
B. the number of unit test failures
C. the percentage of unit test failures
D. the percentage of overall time spent on rework
Answer: D

QUESTION 234

-

You have a GitHub repository.
You create a new repository in Azure DevOps.

You need to recommend a procedure to clone the repository from GitHub to Azure DevOps. What should you recommend?
A. Create a webhook.
B. Create a service connection for GitHub.
C. From Import a Git repository, click Import
D. Create a pull request.
E. Create a personal access token in Azure DevOps.
Answer: C

QUESTION 235
-
You have an Azure DevOps organization named Contoso.
You need to recommend an authentication mechanism that meets the following requirements:
• Supports authentication from Git
• Minimizes the need to provide credentials during authentication What should you recommend?
A. managed identities in Azure Active Directory (Azure AD)
B. personal access tokens (PATs) in Azure DevOps
C. user accounts in Azure Active Directory (Azure AD)
D. Alternate credentials in Azure DevOps
Answer: B

QUESTION 236
Note: This question is part of a series of questions that present the same scenario. Each question in the series contains a unique solution that might meet the stated goals. Some question sets might have more than one correct solution, while others might not have a correct solution.
After you answer a question in this section, you will NOT be able to return to it. As a result, these questions will not appear in the review screen.
You integrate a cloud-hosted Jenkins server and a new Azure DevOps depsoyment. You need Azure DevOps to send a notification to Jenkins when a developer commits changes to a branch in Azure Repos.
Solution: You add a trigger to the build pipeline. Does this meet the goal?
A. Yes
B. NO
Answer: B

QUESTION 237
Note: This question is part of a series of questions that present the same scenario. Each question in the series contains a unique solution that might meet the stated goals. Some question sets might have more than one correct solution, while others might not have a correct solution.
After you answer a question in this section, you will NOT be able to return to it. As a result, these questions will not appear in the review screen.
You have an approval process that contains a condition. The condition requires that releases be approved by a team leader before they are deployed. You have a poky stating that approvals must occur within eight hour.
You discover that deployments fail if the approvals take longer than two hours. You need to ensure that the deployments only fail if the approvals take longer than eight hours.

Solution: From Post-deployment conditions, you modify the Time between reevaluation of gates option. Does this meet the goal?
A. Yes
B. No
Answer: B

QUESTION 238
Note: This question is part of a series of questions that present the same scenario. Each question in the series contains a unique solution that might meet the stated goals. Some question sets might have more than one correct solution, while others might not have a correct solution.
After you answer a question in this section, you will NOT be able to return to it. As a result, these questions will not appear in the review screen.
You have an approval process that contains a condition. The condition requires that releases be approved by a team leader before they are deployed. You have a policy stating that approvals must occur within eight hours.
You discover that deployments fail if the approvals lake longer than two hours. You need to ensure that the deployments only fail if the approvals take longer than eight hours.
Solution: From Pre-deployment conditions, you modify the Timeout setting for predeployment approvals. Does this meet the goal?
A. Yes
B. No
Answer: B

QUESTION 239
Your company has a hybrid cloud between Azure and Azure Stack.
The company uses Azure DevOps for its CI/CD pipelines. Some applications are built by using Erlang and Hack.
You need to ensure that Erlang and Hack are supported as part of the build strategy across the hybrid cloud. The solution must minimize management overhead. What should you use to execute the build pipeline?
A. AzureDevOps self-hosted agents on Azure DevTest Labs virtual machines.
B. AzureDevOps self-hosted agents on virtual machine that run on Azure Stack
C. AzureDevOps self-hosted agents on Hyper-V virtual machines
D. a Microsoft-hosted agent
Answer: B

QUESTION 240
Your company builds a multi tier web application.
You use Azure DevOps and host the production application on Azure virtual machines.
Your team prepares an Azure Resource Manager template of the virtual machine that you mil use to test new features. You need to create a staging environment in Azure that meets the following requirements:
¡E Minimizes the cost of Azure hosting
¡E Provisions the virtual machines automatically
¡E Use* the custom Azure Resource Manager template to provision the virtual machines What should you do?

A. In Azure DevOps, configure new tasks in the release pipeline to create and delete the virtual machines m Azure DevTest Labs.
B. From Azure Cloud Shell, run Azure PowerShell commands to create and delete the new virtual machines in a staging resource group.
C. In Azure DevOps, configure new tasks in the release pipeline to deploy to Azure Cloud Services.
D. In Azure Cloud Shell, run Azure CLI commands to create and delete the new virtual machines in a staging resource group.
Answer: A
A. Mastered
B. Not Mastered
Answer: A

QUESTION 241
Your company plans to use an agile approach to software development You need to recommend an application to provide communication between members of the development team who work in locations around the world. The application must meet the following requirements:
¡E Provide the ability to isolate the members of efferent project teams into separate communication channels and to keep a history of the chats within those channels.
¡E Be available on Windows 10, Mac OS, iOS, and Android operating systems.
¡E Provide the ability to add external contractors and suppliers to projects.
¡E Integrate directly with Azure DevOps. What should you recommend?
A. Octopus
B. Bamboo
C. Microsoft Project
D. Slack
Answer: D

QUESTION 242
Your company uses Azure DevOps for the build pipelines and deployment pipelines of Java based projects. You need to recommend a strategy for managing technical debt.
Which two actions should you include in the recommendation? Each correct answer presents part of the solution NOTE: Each correct selection is worth one point.
A. Integrate Azure DevOps and SonarQube.
B. Integrates Azure DevOPs and Azure DevTest Labs.
C. Configure post-deployment approvals in the deployment pipeline.
D. Configure pre-deployment approvals in the deployment pipelin
Answer: AC

QUESTION 243
Your company has an on-premises Bitbucket Server that is used for Git-based source control. The server is protected by a firewall that blocks inbound Internet traffic.
You plan to use Azure DevOps to manage the build and release processes Which two components are required to integrate Azure DevOps and Bitbucket? Each correct answer presents part of the solution.
NOTE: Each correct selection is worth one port.
A. an External Git service connection

B. a Microsoft hosted agent
C. service hooks
D. a self- hosted agent
E. a deployment M group
Answer: AD

QUESTION 244
Note: This question is part of a series of questions that present the same scenario. Each question in the series contains a unique solution that might meet the stated goals. Some question sets might have more than one correct solution, while others might not have a correct solution.
After you answer a question in this section, you will NOT be able to return to it. As a result, these questions will not appear in the review screen.
Your company has a project in Azure DevOps for a new web application. You need to ensure that when code is checked in, a build runs automatically. Solution: From the Pre-deployment conditions settings of the release pipeline, you select After stage.
Does this meet the goal?
A. Yes
B. No
Answer: B

ONLINE RESOURCES

Practice Paper
Link : https://forms.gle/ufkWNeKm23Zh6aEC9
QR Code :

Video Content
Link :
https://www.youtube.com/playlist?list=PLzlh_31VWEFpyUIe_DuaeIkcThEfMT_BT
QR Code :

Chapter 3: Viva Voce Questions

Q 1: What is Azure DevOps?
Answer: Azure DevOps provides developer services for support teams to plan work, collaborate on code development, and build and deploy applications.
Q 2: How does Azure Pipelines enhance CI/CD processes?
Answer: Azure Pipelines automates the build, testing, and deployment of applications, enabling continuous integration and continuous delivery for projects of any scale and complexity.
Q 3: What is Azure Repos?
Answer: Azure Repos provides Git repositories or Team Foundation Version Control (TFVC) for source control of your code.
Q 4: Can you explain the use of Azure Artifacts?
Answer: Azure Artifacts allows teams to share packages such as NuGet, npm, or Maven from public and private sources and integrate package sharing into their CI/CD pipelines.
Q 5: What role does Azure Test Plans play in DevOps?
Answer: Azure Test Plans provide a suite of tools for testing applications, allowing teams to test early and often to detect and resolve issues quickly, ensuring high-quality releases.
Q 6: Describe the features of Azure Boards.
Answer: Azure Boards deliver a suite of Agile tools to support planning and tracking work, issues, and bugs using Kanban and Scrum methods via customizable dashboards.
Q 7: How does Azure Monitor work in the context of Azure DevOps?
Answer: Azure Monitor collects and analyzes telemetry data from cloud and on-premises environments, helping to understand how applications are performing and proactively identifying issues affecting them.
Q 8: What is Infrastructure as Code (IaC) and how is it implemented in Azure?
Answer: IaC is the management of infrastructure (networks, virtual machines, load balancers, and connection topology) in a descriptive model, using tools like Azure Resource Manager and Terraform.
Q 9: How do you manage secrets in Azure DevOps?
Answer: Secrets management in Azure DevOps can be handled securely using Azure Key Vault, which stores and tightly controls access to tokens, passwords, certificates, API keys, and other secrets.
Q 10: What is the role of Azure Security Center in DevOps?
Answer: Azure Security Center provides unified security management and advanced threat protection across hybrid cloud workloads, integrating security into the DevOps pipeline.
Q 11: Explain the integration of third-party tools with Azure DevOps.
Answer: Azure DevOps supports integration with various third-party tools like Jenkins, Terraform, Ansible, and others, enhancing its flexibility and capability to fit into diverse environments.
Q 12: What is Azure Service Connections?
Answer: Azure Service Connections enable Azure DevOps to connect to external and remote services to fetch or send information, facilitating interactions with other cloud services.
Q 13: How do you use feature flags in Azure DevOps?
Answer: Feature flags in Azure DevOps allow developers to enable or disable features in their applications dynamically without deploying new code, enabling easier testing and faster rollouts.

Q 14: What is Git branching strategy recommended in Azure Repos?
Answer: A common Git branching strategy recommended in Azure Repos is the Git Flow, which includes branches for features, releases, and hotfixes to manage the development and release process effectively.
Q 15: How does Azure handle database versioning in DevOps practices?
Answer: Database versioning in Azure can be managed using SQL Database Projects in Visual Studio and deploying changes through CI/CD pipelines, ensuring consistency across environments.
Q 16: Discuss the use of containers in Azure DevOps.
Answer: Containers in Azure DevOps are used for creating consistent environments for development, testing, and production. Services like Azure Kubernetes Service (AKS) can be used to orchestrate these containers.
Q 17: What is release gating in Azure Pipelines?
Answer: Release gating in Azure Pipelines defines pre-deployment and post-deployment conditions that must be met before continuing with the next phase in the release process, ensuring quality and compliance.
Q 18: How do you automate database deployments in Azure DevOps?
Answer: Automating database deployments can be achieved by integrating tools like SSDT (SQL Server Data Tools) or Redgate SQL Change Automation with Azure DevOps to apply version-controlled changes to the database.
Q 19: Explain rollback mechanisms in Azure DevOps.
Answer: Rollback mechanisms in Azure DevOps involve using deployment strategies that allow quick reversion to a previous version of the application if a new release fails or introduces bugs.
Q 20: How is user feedback managed in Azure DevOps?
Answer: User feedback is managed through Azure Boards, where feedback can be linked directly to work items, allowing teams to prioritize and track user suggestions and issues effectively.

YouTube Link for Viva Voce QUESTIONs:
https://www.youtube.com/playlist?list=PLzlh 31VWEFooExmWXGmW-qO6wqfPTSm3

QR Code:

YouTube Videos Playlists for all Microsoft Certifications Videos

Microsoft Azure AI Fundamentals AZ-900
Link: https://www.youtube.com/playlist?list=PLzlh 31VWEFq9KU8Gr0ISbfj-TW6k17f8

QR Code:

Microsoft Azure Administrator AZ-104 Microsoft Azure Virtual Desktop AZ-140
Link: https://www.youtube.com/playlist?list=PLzlh 31VWEFq7JHJMuPJZcw-XShaPrUYP

QR Code:

Microsoft Azure Virtual Desktop AZ-140
Link: https://www.youtube.com/playlist?list=PLzlh_31VWEFowmPK_ro41wiljGoGKexGI
QR Code:

Microsoft Azure Developer AZ-204
Link:
https://www.youtube.com/playlist?list=PLzlh_31VWEFqT72UPVCUi6rqRqLBuwMSr
QR Code:

Designing Microsoft Azure Infrastructure Solution AZ-305
Link:
https://www.youtube.com/playlist?list=PLzlh_31VWEFpTerOknh9kgL4eTbhQwDND
QR Code:

Microsoft Azure Devops Engineer AZ-400
Link: https://www.youtube.com/playlist?list=PLzlh_31VWEFpyUIe_DuaeIkcThEfMT_BT
QR Code:

Microsoft Azure Security Engineer AZ-500
Link:
https://www.youtube.com/playlist?list=PLzlh_31VWEFqFBJgQTPNucIO0wVJdjNmS
QR Code:

Microsoft Azure Network Engineer AZ-700
Link:
https://www.youtube.com/playlist?list=PLzlh_31VWEFowujgDl16YDCvsQtmKgEqL
QR Code:

Microsoft Azure Fundamentals AZ-900

Link: https://www.youtube.com/playlist?list=PLzlh_31VWEFpeXZ2p32R1zDsgcbV8kI1K

QR Code:

Microsoft Azure Data Engineer DP-203

Link: https://www.youtube.com/playlist?list=PLzlh_31VWEFp3XTNqoS60UAOzl8NVG-5z

QR Code:

Microsoft Azure Database Administrator DP- 300

Link: https://www.youtube.com/playlist?list=PLzlh_31VWEFpv-rmc2mbpoIqUOqVW_cIo

QR Code: